THE BLOCKBUSTER TOY!

THE BLOCKBUSTER TOY! How to Invent the Next BIG Thing

By Gene Del Vecchio

Illustrations by
Roderick Fong

PELICAN PUBLISHING COMPANY
Gretna 2003

The word "Pelican" and the depiction of a pelican are trademarks
of Pelican Publishing Company, Inc., and are registered
in the U.S. Patent and Trademark Office.

Library of Congress Cataloging-in-Publication Data

Del Vecchio, Gene.
  The blockbuster toy! : how to invent the next big thing / by Gene
Del Vecchio ; illustrations by Roderick Fong.
      p. cm.
  ISBN 1-58980-122-9 (hardcover : alk. paper)
1. Toys—Marketing. 2. Toy making. 3. Advertising. I. Title.
  HD9993.T692D45 2003
  688.7'2'0685—dc22
                                        2003014903

*The toys whose names are capitalized in this book are those that, to the author's
and publisher's knowledge, are likely claimed as trademarks by their manufacturers or others. This is whether or not they are accompanied by a trademark
symbol. Some toys in this book do carry trademark symbols. In these few cases,
it was a requirement stipulated by certain companies in order to obtain photographs of their toys.*

Printed in the United States of America
Published by Pelican Publishing Company, Inc.
1000 Burmaster Street, Gretna, Louisiana 70053

Contents

Acknowledgments

I wish to thank the companies and institutions that provided photographs, statements from executives, or a combination of both. These included the Allard Pierson Museum in Amsterdam, Arvin Design, Bandai America Incorporated, Binney & Smith, Duncan Toy Company, Fisher-Price, Lionel L.L.C., Litzky Public Relations, Marvel, Mattel, Meccano, MGA Entertainment Inc., the National Museum of American History at the Smithsonian, Original Appalachian Artworks Inc., Pleasant Company, Seven Towns Ltd, Sony, Sony Online Entertainment, Strottman International, Toy Biz, Toy Industry Association, Uncle Milton Industries Inc., The Walt Disney Company, the *Washington Post,* and Wham-O.

I also want to thank Lucky J. Meisenheimer, M.D., for providing a photo from his personal collection of yo-yos.

A special thank you goes to Craig Spitzer, vice-president of marketing research at Fisher-Price. He provided many wonderful suggestions on an early manuscript.

I want to thank Pelican Publishing for providing the idea for this book and for their continued, gracious support.

A special thank you must also go to Roderick Fong, who provided the wonderful illustrations that help bring each chapter to life.

Finally, I want to thank Linda, Matthew, and Megan.

THE BLOCKBUSTER TOY!

CHAPTER 1

A Toymaker's Life

A Brief History of Toys

After toiling all day in the hot sun, making his meager living as a farmer, a father residing along the mighty Huang He River in China walked with his eight-year-old son into a windswept field. The father paused; a strong breeze upon his face told him that the conditions were near optimal. He smiled as he knelt on the ground and unfurled a bundle that he had held tightly beneath his arm. The contents of the bundle fell gently to the earth. His son's eyes suddenly danced with delight as his tiny fingers grabbed at the unexpected treasure. The boy pulled at the gift, made of a light bamboo frame and a silk sail, a project his father and mother had been working to complete for many weeks with materials not easy to acquire. That made it all the more precious.

The father gave his son a string that was attached to the contraption, told him to wait there, and then he walked across the field with the silk and wooden design, the light material billowing slightly in the breeze. The father turned and paused when he reached the other end of the field, waiting for the breeze to strengthen just a bit. As it did, the father tossed the contraption into the air and it soared upward and seemingly above all of China. The boy screamed with delight as he kept a strong grip on the string, holding the kite firmly as it rose. The kite's silk revealed the painting of a fierce dragon. The small boy had seen only a couple of other kites in his entire life, often used by nearby army camps to send coded messages back and forth across China. But now he had one of his own, not for the military uses of adults but for the amusement of children.

In the modern calendar, the year that this father and son walked into the field was 1000 B.C., some three thousand years ago. This was some five hundred years before the birth of the great philosopher Confucius, long before the first Qin emperor, Shi Huangdi, ordered the construction of the Great Wall, and nearly a thousand years before Buddhism was introduced into China from India.

The simple kite was among the first blockbuster toys. It was not mass produced by an international corporation, not announced with the aid of a multimillion-dollar advertising blitz, and certainly not discovered in the bottom of a fast-food bag. It was constructed, announced, and distributed by loving parents.

Far to the west, a small boy and his sister lived in the comfort born of kings. Their diet was rich in beef, antelope, and gazelle meat. They ate many finely baked goods and drank fruit beverages obtained from plants that grew along the mighty Nile River. While these children were more modestly dressed, their parents adorned themselves with rare jewelry, fine clothes, and brightly colored cosmetics. The children had a rich life with many diversions. Playthings were often crafted by others for their amusement. The boy played with a toy tiger, its mouth opening and closing on hinges as the child pulled a string. He had long since given up his rattle, which was shaped like a cow with stones inside. But he still played with his miniature wheeled horses that he loved to race across his palace's intricately painted tile floor. His sister often played with these as well, though her favorite possession was a doll with moveable arms, made of painted wood and wearing a short white dress. Sadly, this girl, the daughter of Pharaoh, died and was

Two horses (modern wheels). Egypt, Naukratis, sixth century B.C. Courtesy of the Allard Pierson Museum, Amsterdam.

buried at Thebes with that doll. These were the Egyptians who lived several thousand years ago. They gave civilization many things, including a paperlike material for writing known as papyrus and the 365-day calendar.

In a temple farther to the east, a group of children clad in simple woolen garments scampered through a ceremonial dwelling after religious services had ended. They were taking turns pulling their carved-limestone playthings across the stone floor. One of the toys was in the shape of a lion, whereas another was in the shape of a porcupine. They were both mounted on wheels and pulled with a string, making them among the first-known pull toys in the history of the world. The children chased each other out through the dwelling's large doors, and in so doing, they inadvertently left their playthings behind.

Later that evening, they forgot entirely where they had placed them, and the toys were left to be found thousands of years later. This was Iran and the temple is now 3,000 years old.

Back again to the west some years later, another civilization was approaching the height of its golden age. In one of this culture's city-states, a small family consisting of two parents and their son and daughter worked their modest though prosperous farm. It was a hard but rewarding life. They raised pigs, cultivated a small grove of olives, grew wheat and barley, and even worked a few fine crafts. And though they might appear to be laborers alone, the spirit of these people would ignite a world. They were fiercely independent and creative thinkers. Their minds constantly examined nature and existence on both a grand and subtle level.

One particular evening, as the family retreated to their four-room house built of sun-dried bricks, the mother was busy polishing the edges of a small disk-shaped object that she had made from terracotta clay. She smiled as she paused to feel the smooth edges.

"Mama, is it ready?" asked her seven-year-old daughter.

"Yes, it is!" her mother said proudly as she handed her the disk. "But be careful," she cautioned. "This one is made of clay and is more delicate than your wooden one."

The child took the disk, which was beautifully painted by her mother's own hand, and as she had done so many times before with the other she owned, she let it drop to the floor. But just as the disk almost touched, she gave a good yank on a string that catapulted it up again. And so it went again, up and down. It was a yo-yo.

"That's enough," said her mother. "Remember, this one is not for playing. When you come of age, we will offer this toy of your youth to the gods, as is our custom, so as to mark your rite of passage into adulthood." The mother smiled as she took the delicately crafted yo-yo from her daughter and carefully set it down in a place of honor near the fire. The daughter retreated to the corner of their cottage with her younger brother and began to play with assorted other diversions that her mother and father had crafted. They included a clay doll with moveable arms that held a rattle in each hand, a top, and a hollowed-out wooden horse that carried small wooden warriors within its belly . . . the fabled Trojan horse.

This was the year 500 B.C. The farm was near Athens, the very cradle of western civilization, law, and medicine. It will be 200 more years before the Greek philosopher Plato founds a school known as the Academy. This is the land where rudimentary forms of government will influence the world to this very day, where Aristotle will enlighten the minds of mankind and be the mentor to Alexander the Great, and where ancient religious festivals will become the foundation of the celebrated Olympics.

Spinning top. Terracotta. Greece, fourth century B.C. Courtesy of the Allard Pierson Museum, Amsterdam.

Jointed doll with rattles in hands, from a child's tomb. Terracotta. Athens, Greece, ca. 450 B.C. Courtesy of the Allard Pierson Museum, Amsterdam.

Children even farther to the west, in the year A.D. 79, sat playing with toy soldiers and marionettes. They imagined great battles and fantasized about being great warriors and generals. After all, their civilization had come to conquer the known world, and it was often said that the sun never set on this civilization, for its depth and breadth was immense. These children were Romans, and each had a relative who was part of the Roman legions, taught to conquer or be conquered. As such, many of the playthings constructed for these children were not just for amusement, but a way to introduce them to the sometimes harsh realities of the world. But on this particular day, as these children ran through the streets of their town, tragedy would befall them far too early. They were in the shadow of a mountain that would spell their demise. Mount Vesuvius erupted, and due to a wind that blew in their direction instead of another, they were buried along with their beloved Pompeii. Years later, their toys would be unearthed, along with hollowed-out forms in the ash where their bodies once were.

In a New World, by Old World standards, children ran about their village, playing many games. Girls played with dolls fashioned from cornhusks and with feather-stuffed leather balls. Boys played with miniature bows and arrows and longed for the day when they would be asked to accompany the men on the buffalo hunt, a very important rite of passage. They would use the leather of the beast to make fine garments and the meat to fill their bellies. These were great, proud peoples who had become as one with nature. They were the Native Americans, and they dominated this land many hundreds of years before Europeans set foot upon the so-called New World.

This is all to say that toys are as old as mankind. They were there at great moments in history and all the moments in between, all around the world. They are part of us and, in many ways, define us. Throughout the years, toys reflected our religions, environments, and passions. They revealed what we feared, what we sought to achieve, how we made a living, and what we dreamed. Though the finer details of the stories cited above were created to paint a rich mosaic, the toys and each general situation were based upon the archaeological record. It was real.

"Toys have been uncovered in every part of the world from India to Peru, and in every era, dating back 5,000 years," says Dr. Annemarieke Willemsen, curator of the National Museum of Antiquities of the Netherlands and author of *Kinder delijt* (*Children's Delight: Medieval Toys in the Netherlands,* Nijmegen, 1998). She went on to tell me:

> They were prominent because they played an important role in children's lives. Yes . . . they were often for a child's amusement. These playthings might include ancient spinning tops, yo-yos, hoops, knucklebones, and rattles. Among the oldest and most consistent are animal figures on wheels, with a hole in the nose for a string to pull them. But toys also helped prepare children for life's challenges, and they mirrored the society that produced them. Boys in ancient Pompeii played with figures of Roman soldiers and gladiators. Girls in ancient Egypt, Greece, and Rome played with moveable figurines of adult women. . . . Jointed dolls and wheeled horses can be considered the bestsellers of antiquity. They were made in large quantities and regularly given as presents. In their style and decoration, toys of all ancient periods unveiled the fashion of their times.

This is not to say that all children in all times benefited from such playthings. Certainly, children in families with greater means had more toys. It's also true that, for many thousands of years, childhood was not recognized as a time for play but simply as a time before these younger adults would be pressed into service to help their families make an adult living. Still, even before childhood emerged as a special time, there were indications that many began to view it as such. It should also be noted that, throughout history, toys were constructed for the amusement of adults, and many of those playthings have been unearthed.

For thousands of years, toys meant for the young were undoubtedly created by parents and relatives using materials available in nature. They lovingly crafted figures, dolls, balls, marbles, tops, and many other items for the amusement of their children. It was a giving and sharing of love that spanned eons.

Though parents were important early toymakers, it is also clear that independent craftsmen were involved at very early times. Archaeologists unearthed a toy factory that existed in India some five thousand years ago. As civilization began to mature and move slowly from a predominantly hunting, gathering, and even farming existence to one that included craftsmanship of many kinds, parents' involvement in creating playthings gradually subsided as these professional toymakers began to appear. But it was undoubtedly a haphazard process, and only those with greater means could afford to buy a plaything from a craftsman.

Fairs across Europe during the Middles Ages brought craftsmen from near and far to sell their goods. Carved figures of knights and horses were common in the toy box. The hobbyhorse made its first appearance. German toymakers began to refine their craft and became master toymakers, drawing heavily upon quality materials found in the Black Forest.

A toy shop in Boston, one of the first known in the New World, appeared in the early 1700s. "When I was a child of seven years old," wrote Benjamin Franklin, "my friends, on a holiday, filled my pocket with coppers. I went directly to a shop where they sold toys for children, and being charmed with the sound of a whistle, that I met by way in the hands of another boy, I voluntarily offered and gave all my money for one."

In the late 1700s, craftsmen began to add another dimension to toys: mechanical and clockwork movements. A Swiss watchmaker created a doll that could move and, with writing implement in hand, actually write words. A French inventor, who created the metronome for the piano, decided to use his

talents to make the first speaking doll in the 1820s. When its
arms were positioned just right, it said, *"Maman"* and *"Papa."*
American toymakers began creating toy trains and figures that
moved by the power of a key-wound spring. When gun manufacturing slowed down after the Civil War, one manufacturer
invented the cap gun as a way to sustain production. The BB
gun followed by 1886.

The Industrial Revolution allowed for mass production,
which drove prices down and made manufactured toys far
more accessible to all. They were often made of cast iron and
tin, using the mass-production techniques and cheap materials
of the period. American tin toys became world famous by the
late 1800s and early 1900s, during which time factories produced millions of tin toys such as trains, fire engines, wagons,
and figures.

Toys' Emergence into Pop Culture

Today's brands began to appear in the early 1900s. These
included Lionel Trains (1901), Crayola Crayons (1903),
Erector Sets (1913), and Tinkertoy (1913). Donald Duncan
reignited the yo-yo in the late 1920s.

The mid-1900s saw more advancement in creating and selling toys. Plastics began to replace metal and wood. Mass distributors replaced mom-and-pop toy stores. Mass marketing
replaced random newspaper advertisements.

Ole Christiansen invented the early prototype of LEGO
Building Bricks in 1949. Ruth Handler, the cofounder of
Mattel, invented the Barbie doll in 1959. Two brothers named
Henry and Helal Hassenfeld founded Hasbro, which in 1964
introduced an American icon, the G.I. Joe action figure. And
while we think of these companies as global enterprises of
some might, it's important to remember that they each began
as a one- or two-person operation, often at a toymaker's bench,
in search of a plaything to make a child smile.

But nothing could have predicted what happened in 1955.

That was a landmark year for toys. That's when Mattel paid $500,000 to advertise its products on "The Mickey Mouse Club." It was the year that mass marketing found a mass audience. The marketing of toys entered a new era, and so did toymakers. What had been a cottage industry for thousands of years transformed into one with huge dimensions. Once toys found a place on television, they became an enduring part of pop culture, not only reflecting the times on a massive scale but creating the fads as well.

Money began to change hands on an unprecedented scale and toys became big business. Total toy advertising expenditures in the United States in 2001 approached $790 million, the bulk of which was on television, according to CMR/TNS Media Intelligence U.S. and Publishers Information Bureau. The total dollar sales of toys in the United States reached $34 billion that year, including both traditional toys and video games, according to the NPD Group and the Toy Industry Association. Worldwide sales of toys were roughly $70 billion. The American International TOY FAIR became the industry's annual event where many toy companies come to showcase their new toys and attract buyers such as Wal-Mart and Toys R Us. The 2003 TOY FAIR, which is owned and managed by the Toy Industry Association, hosted some 1,700 toy exhibitors and over 11,000 buyers from around the world. The development of this forum, plus manufacturers' private toy shows, was significant because toys gained both status and an international stage. Year in and year out, the toy trade, the media, and the consuming public actively wait for the Next Big Thing in toys, that item that will ignite sales, passions, and pop culture.

And so, each and every year, toymakers ponder how to create the Next Big Thing. This haunts them, for the elusive answer has created both fortunes and disasters. Why are some toys immensely successful and others not? Why do children ask parents for some toys and ignore thousands of others? What is the role of parents, and why do they accept some toys and not allow

2003 American International TOY FAIR. Courtesy of the Toy Industry Association.

others? And what is it, beyond the mere making and selling of a toy, that can bring it to blockbuster status today? Promotion and public relations engines, for example, have recently added mightily to the power of advertising. Entertainment plays a critical role, too, as more and more toys are born not from a toymaker's bench as much as they are born from a screenwriter's pen.

Still, there are no guarantees. The dark truth is that there are more failures than successes in the toy world. Many new toys don't make it past one selling season, and most new toy companies eventually evaporate. Why?

The Blockbuster Toy

The Blockbuster Toy! will attempt to answer these questions. It's a journey into the very birth of the massive toy brands that exist today in order to help the reader better understand how and why they came into being. It will provide keen insights into why children love certain toys year after year and why parents accept them year after year. The objective of this book is to help today's toymakers achieve even greater success and to help toymaker wannabes ignite a career and sustain it.

Through our journey, it is humbling to keep one thing in mind; that in the history of the world, toys were rarely about gaining riches and fame, an unfortunate side effect of contemporary times. Instead, toys were about sharing love and igniting laughter. They were crafted by parents and a handful of artisans in hopes of creating a smile on a child's face. In turn, that would make the parents happy, too, because it allowed them to entertain their beloved children in a world often filled with too many harsh realities.

Don't follow the money. Follow the smile. This is not just a sentimental directive; it's also a financially astute one. Following the elements that inspire children to smile will ensure that your toys are satisfying children's core emotional needs. It's also the case that many toymakers who invented blockbuster toys did so by not following the pack (i.e., the money). Instead, they followed new paths that had yet to demonstrate their financial worth. They satisfied emotional needs that other toymakers had ignored. They found ways to produce smiles that others missed.

So follow the smiles. That was, and remains, the ultimate value of a blockbuster toy. Following the smiles will help you invent the Next Big Thing that millions of children and parents will embrace for generations. With that in mind, let us begin.

CHAPTER 2

The Essence of a Blockbuster Toy

Most new toys never live beyond a single year. Far fewer are still on the shelf the year after that, demonstrating that the toy industry is more often about eventual failure than sustained success. Yet every year, thousands of new toys vie for the attention of millions of children and their parents. "Buy me! Buy me!" shout the multitude of toy commercials on television and packages on store shelves. Yet there are far more toys than dollars to buy them, allowing consumers to be more selective now than during any other time in history. Many people outside the industry, however, mistakenly believe that toy manufacturers are as successful as Pied Pipers, playing a tune that children and parents follow obediently to the enrichment of toymakers everywhere. But everyone in the industry knows the truth: children and their parents are more often in charge, running about while executives try to catch up with them long enough to get their toys noticed. And so, many toys and toy-industry executives each year end up as road kill, as children and parents veer off to obtain someone else's playthings.

It is tough to make a great toy. It is tougher to get that toy noticed. It is tougher still to actually get inside a child's toy box once. It is nearly impossible to get inside that toy box again and again, year after year. The few toys that do are special, indeed, because their inventors knew, or stumbled upon, some secret formula that helped their toys reach Next Big Thing status.

The Blockbuster Toys

Which toys are blockbusters? I confer this status on toys that meet either of two criteria:

• Type 1 Toys, The Evergreens: These toys link generations and become an enduring part of kid culture. They were played with by parents when they were children, and many parents like to introduce their children to the same. A prime example is the Barbie doll. Evergreens are special because they have found a way to survive decades. This is a significant accomplishment in the toy business.

• Type 2 Toys, The Flash: These toys tend to burst onto the pop culture scene, sometimes based upon the launch of a new movie. They reach dizzying heights and then fizzle to far lower levels or completely vanish. Type 2 toys also include toys that gained a lot of attention because of their fresh new perspective, but they too eventually decline. A recent example might include the Furby.

The greatest riches often go to Type 1 blockbusters because they are continued successes, providing a continuous source of revenue for the toymaker and, more importantly, a continuous stream of smiles from children. But both types of blockbuster successes are worth review, because their developers found a way to capture the attention of an entire world. These toys often created new categories, introduced new ways of thinking about toys, or provided new approaches to marketing toys. They possessed a quality that inspired a multitude of children to declare, "I want that!" even though these children were faced with thousands of other options. These toys possessed an equally powerful quality that led parents to respond, "Okay!"

The list of the honored blockbuster toys is in exhibit 1. They span the years 1900 through the early 2000s. You will see an abundance of Type 1 Evergreens born in the early years (e.g., LEGO bricks, Barbie doll). There are more Type 2 toys born in the 1970s and later undoubtedly because of the rise

Exhibit 1
The Blockbuster Toys!
(Estimated date of toy release)

1900's
1901 Lionel Trains
1903 Crayola Crayons
1903 Teddy Bear

1910's
1912 Cracker Jack (Toys/Prizes)
1913 Erector Set
1913 Tinkertoy Construction Set

1920's
1924 Lincoln Logs Building Sets
1929 Duncan Yo-Yo

1930's
1930 Mickey Mouse (Toys)
1934 Monopoly Game
1935 Raggedy Ann Doll
1939 View-Master

1940's
1945 Slinky
1947 Tonka Trucks
1947 Magic 8 Ball
1949 Automatic Binding Bricks
(forerunner of Lego Bricks)

1950's
1950's Army Men Figures
1950 Silly Putty
1952 PEZ Candy (Toy Dispensers)
1952 Mr. Potato Head
1954 Matchbox
1956 Play-Doh Modeling Compound
1956 Uncle Milton's Ant Farm Brand Habitats
1958 Hula Hoop Brand Hoops
1958 Frisbee Disc
1959 Barbie Doll

1960's
1960 Etch A Sketch
1960 Instant Life Kit (Sea Monkeys)
1963 Easy-Bake Oven
1964 G.I. Joe
1964 Creepy Crawlers (Thingmaker)
1965 Superball
1965 Operation Skill Game
1965 See 'n Say (The Farmer Says)
1965 Spirograph Design Toy
1966 Rock'em Sock'em Robots
1967 Battleship Naval Combat Game
1968 Hot Wheels
1969 Nerf Ball

1970's
1970 Little Tikes
1977 The Rubik's Cube
1977 Atari Video Game System
1977 Star Wars (Toys)
1977 Klutz Books and Guides
1978 McDonald's Happy Meal (Toys)
1979 Strawberry Shortcake Doll
1979 Intellivision Video Game System

1980's
1981 Masters of the Universe (He-Man)
1982 Cabbage Patch Kids
1984 Transformers
1985 Nintendo Entertainment System
1985 Teddy Ruxpin
1985 Pound Puppies
1986 The American Girls Collection
1988 Teenage Mutant Ninja Turtles
1989 Super Soaker
1989 Game Boy Video Game System
1989 Batman (Toys)

1990's
1993 Mighty Morphin Power Rangers
1993 MYST Computer Game
1993 The Beanie Babies Collection
1996 Tickle Me Elmo
1996 Tomb Raider Video Game
1996 Tamagotchi Virtual Pet
1997 Build-A-Bear Workshop
1998 Furby
1998 Rescue Heroes
1998 Pokemon (for Game Boy)
1999 EverQuest Online Game
1999 LeapPad Learning System

2000's
2001 Bratz Dolls
2001 Beyblade High Performance Tops
2001 Bionicle (Lego Building Toy)
2002 Spider-Man (Toys)

> Note: We respectfully note that the great majority of these toys are claimed as trademarks by manufacturers or others.

of entertainment properties that come and go, as well as the rise of one-hit wonders. Though they are not strictly toys, some notable games such as Monopoly, Battleship, and the more recent EverQuest are included in the exhibit because much can be gained from examining these successes.

A couple of caveats are worth pointing out. Firstly, I did not categorize transportation vehicles as toys, such as skating-related brands (e.g., Rollerblade), bicycle-related brands (e.g., Schwinn), skateboarding-related brands (e.g., Hobie), wagon-related brands (e.g., Radio Flyer), or scooter-related brands (e.g., Razor). These are certainly blockbusters, but they go well beyond the toy designation. Secondly, there are undoubtedly other blockbuster toys and games you remember from your youth or even work on today that are not on the list. This was not so much oversight as it was brevity. What we learn of from toys in exhibit 1 applies to all blockbusters.

The Six Qualities of a Blockbuster

Using a content review of the toys in exhibit 1, insights by noted industry experts, and my twenty-plus years in youth marketing, I developed a list of the six core qualities that help toys achieve blockbuster status. Though some of these may seem obvious, they were not so obvious to the thousands of toymakers whose products have failed. These qualities will be discussed throughout the rest of the book.

• *Blockbuster toys best satisfy a child's deeply rooted emotional needs.* They are said to be *on emotional target.* They do not skim along the surface of emotional needs. Instead, they create a connection with a multitude of children by fulfilling their deepest needs. They provide key features and play patterns that fulfill these needs better than other toys did previously. These include the child's need for:

Pride
Self-Esteem

Appreciation/Attention
Accomplishment/Mastery
Creativity
Beauty
Power/Empowerment
Control
Silliness/Grossness
Independence/Freedom (harmless rebellion)
Belonging
Love/Nurturing
Security
Fear Reduction/Bravery
Sensory Gratification
Mental and Physical Development
Fantasy Fulfillment
Hunger/Thirst

If these needs sound familiar, they should. They are the needs all of us share. The toys that do the best job at satisfying these needs are well on their way to achieving blockbuster status. A four-year-old child who draws a splendid picture of her family with the brand of Crayola Crayons will feel creative and accomplished and proud indeed, especially when her parents display her work of art prominently upon the refrigerator door. A seven-year-old boy who imagines he is Spider-Man in order to thwart evil in the world will feel empowered by this strong fantasy. These are not small issues for the child but strong and enduring ones.

The fulfillment of these deep emotional needs is the *fun* that creates the *smile!* Unfortunately, too many toymakers look for fun in the random gimmicks and laser lights while ignoring the core emotional drivers. But toymakers who build unique features and play patterns into their toys with the single-minded purpose of better fulfilling a child's emotional needs are more likely to succeed. Many times this can be accomplished by using innovative technology to "plus" toys, making common ones special in ways that better fulfill children's needs. The question to ask, then, is not how to make toys fun or different for their own sake, but rather, how to make toys that satisfy deep emotional needs in ways that have not been achieved. There are two potential paths: create a toy that has key features and play patterns that fulfill an emotional need that other toy-makers have ignored in a given category, or fulfill the same needs others have but do it better.

• *Blockbuster toys achieve general parent acceptance.* It is important to remember that a parent's needs should be taken into account in order to be on emotional target. Toys that can best fulfill one or more of a parent's desires tend to achieve block-buster status. These needs include the following:

Child's Happiness
Child's Continued Enjoyment (play value)
Child's Creativity
Child's Safety
Child's Mental and Physical Development
Child's Success
Child's Health
Child's Love

This is a matter of providing qualities that parents can readily appreciate. Certainly, parents can appreciate blockbuster toys such as Crayola Crayons because they help inspire the child's creativity. Parents can also appreciate Fisher-Price preschool toys because they help foster a child's early development. And though some parents may object to Spider-Man's use of force to thwart bad guys, many will appreciate Spider-Man and the associated toys for the gentle fantasy that it is, while recalling their own youthful connection with the character. However, if a toy is considered rather inappropriate and not in keeping with the values that parents regard highly, the parents as gatekeepers will take over, and the toy's chances of making it into the toy box will be diminished.

A parent's own needs can sometimes be in conflict. Some parents, for example, may dislike certain toys because they consider them to be mildly inappropriate for their children, but their concern is overshadowed by the happiness that the toy will bring to these children. Toys that are "gross" often fall into this category. Most boys love them. Some moms are annoyed by them. But many parents will tolerate them for the sake of their child's happiness, while knowing that such toys are a part of youthful experiences and expressions. It's also true that the child's desires become more important in the marketer's world when the child is old enough to voice opinions to the parent. Balancing a child's needs with a parent's needs will be discussed in later chapters, but for now, it is enough to know that a toy's potential for success is enhanced greatly when it satisfies both the child's and parent's emotional needs better than other toy brands have to date.

• *Some blockbuster toys rise to prominence because they perfectly align with significant historical events or societal trends.* They are said to be *on trend.* Some toys, for example, rose to immense heights because they were introduced at a time of war (e.g., Army Men), the Great Depression (e.g., Monopoly Game), the emergence of industrialization (e.g., Erector Set), or grand shifts in society such as the greater empowerment of women (e.g., Barbie doll). Such toymakers had keen insights into the times in which they lived and thus crafted toys that fit massively emerging needs or attitudes. Some of these toys not only rose on the crest of these great waves, but they continued to ride those waves through multiple generations of children because they were enjoyed by parents when they were young, too. For today's toymaker, the question is this: what are the current massive events and societal trends that can help you invent tomorrow's Next Big Thing? This, too, will be examined in this book.

- *Blockbuster toys are often regenerative.* Many toys have achieved sustained success (Type 1) because they not only satisfy timeless emotional needs as outlined earlier, but they do so in ways that continually connect with current fads. They were built in a way that allowed them to easily reinvent themselves. They are said to be *regenerative.* The Barbie doll fulfills the need to aspire and to experiment with life's potential, but the Barbie doll is reinvented year after year to reflect a girl's current aspirations. When little girls wanted to be nurses, Barbie was a nurse. When little girls broadened their goals, Barbie accommodated, becoming a doctor, astronaut, and even president of the United States. In that way, she remains both timeless and timely, reflecting the changes in society but in ways that connect with a deep emotional need to aspire and achieve. In my earlier book, *Creating Ever-Cool: A Marketer's Guide to a Kid's Heart,* I called such brands *Ever-Cools* because they perfectly captured the formula to stay cool year after year. When developing new toys, toymakers need to ask themselves if their toy can be easily updated to reflect shifts in trends and pop culture. Toys that can more easily reinvent themselves have greater blockbuster potential. These will be discussed throughout this book as well.

- *Blockbuster toys often have significant* playful *marketing efforts behind them.* The success of toys in today's world often depends upon the effectiveness of the manufacturer's marketing efforts (advertising, promotion, public relations, etc.). In many ways, the marketing must be as engaging and playful as the toy, and so toymakers must have an expertise in many elements of marketing. If not, then a "potential" blockbuster toy on the toymaker's bench may never make it to blockbuster status in the world. It's also true that, beyond a toymaker's own efforts, success can be related to a toymaker's alliance with the right corporate partners (e.g., movie studios, fast-food restaurants, etc.). As competition has grown over the past few years, toy manufacturers have found it helpful to develop toys based upon entertainment properties that offer an alliance with high-spending partners. It's often a decision made by dollars. If you're making a toy with the imprint of a character on it, your toy may benefit greatly if that character is supported with advertising dollars spent by others to introduce the movie, the fast-food meal, and the ride at the amusement park. The immense spending will provide a halo effect over the toy, and you can, at least theoretically, spend less on advertising than you would need to without corporate partners. Of course, you have to pay a sizeable royalty to the company that owns the franchise, but it can be safer than trying to create a character of your own. However, it is also the case that many toy manufacturers have been burned of late when the movies that introduced the characters flopped. Even if the movie is successful, it may not lead to enough toy sales to meet immense expectations. Still, alliance partners remain an important part of today's toy realities, and the odds of success might increase significantly if a toy manufacturer aligns with the right piece of entertainment that lends itself to toys that fulfill needs. All of this will be discussed.

• *Some blockbuster toys reach such status because of the* "X Factor." This is the event that no one can foresee, and yet it can have a dramatic impact on a toy's rise to prominence. It does happen, given the scope and power of mass media, that a toy can be catapulted into the stratosphere because a celebrity fell in love with it and then fawned over the plaything on a nationally televised talk show. It has also happened that some toys reached blockbuster status not solely because of their innate appeal, per se, but because rumor spread of their shortage, which fueled greater interest and demand, which fueled more media coverage, more shortage, and eventual blockbuster status. The power of mass media cannot be underestimated. Such cases will be examined as well.

Central Principles

This book will probe deeply into the reasons why certain toys attain blockbuster status, using the aforementioned qualities of best fulfilling a child's and/or parent's needs (*on emotional target*), aligning with significant historical events and societal trends (*on trend*), being capable of easily reinventing itself (*regenerative*), developing an effective marketing program (*playful marketing*), and even the occurrence of random events (*X Factor*). Not all blockbuster toys meet all of these qualities, but toys that achieved several of them quite well, particularly fulfilling core emotional needs, increased their chances of becoming and staying blockbusters. Throughout the book we will highlight which of the above qualities certain blockbuster toys seemed to possess that helped them rise to blockbuster status.

But an analysis of exhibit 1 reveals something more. The most wildly successful blockbusters had two essential elements in common, and in a way, they united many of the aforementioned qualities of a blockbuster.

• *A blockbuster toy is a powerful catalyst.* It possesses qualities that create a deep reaction within the child and thus *transform* the child in a wondrous way, either in fantasy or reality. Tinkertoy construction sets *transform* children into creators. Fisher-Price preschool toys *transform* children into achievers and accomplished masters. Cabbage Patch Kids *transform* girls in fantasy into caring mothers. G.I. Joe action figures *transform* boys in fantasy into warriors who will defend freedom. This is no small thing. It is at the very bedrock of all blockbuster toys. Through effective use of unique features and play patterns, the blockbusters were more able to bring out a persona that already existed within the child than nonblockbuster toys could. All of this transformation may, in fact, happen in one afternoon as the child skips from one blockbuster toy to the next, one persona to the next. Blockbuster toys transform children in wonderful ways by helping them enter worlds in order to experiment with life's options.

Blockbuster toys *transform* children. It's a subtle but power-ful idea. I know this firsthand, having researched children and their play for over two decades and across hundreds of studies. The blockbuster toys have a way of immediately pulling chil-dren into fantasy worlds. Observing from behind a mirror, I often watched as children were allowed to play with block-buster toys by themselves—at least they could not see the adults watching from behind the mirror. Left supposedly alone, many children would begin to talk, often to the block-buster toys, as the fantasies in their minds began to build. The rest of the real world would instantly vanish. In moments of grandeur, the children would invent imaginary friends or foes, get on their stomachs to view the environment from the toy's point of view, jump to their feet to defend Earth, do a victory lap in an imaginary stadium as they mastered a skill, or hug a baby doll and speak to it in sweet whispers. When the adult interviewer reentered the room, the window to the children's personas and fantasies would suddenly shut tight, and the chil-dren would become children once again.

This was in stark contrast to toys that were not blockbusters. Children would play with them for a bit, often with one inter-esting feature, get tired of them quickly, and then begin to play with another toy. Such toys had little play value. That's because the nonblockbusters did not have the *right* features that led to *enduring* play patterns, which connected with *deep emotional drivers,* which in turn enticed the child's persona to come out as if saying, "Come play with me and be transformed into a hero, or mother, or master, or whatever." Those toys that achieve blockbuster status typically attain it because they did the *best* job in helping children transform in unique ways. As stated earlier, they have the cues and features that truly help children feel more like mothers, more like heroes, and more.

The following chapters discuss the key types of transforma-tions that blockbuster toys have achieved, and how they did it through features, benefits, and play patterns that help children attain, as never before, a heightened sense of transformation. These include transforming a child into a master, creator, nurturer, emulator, friend, collector, story lover, and experience seeker. These paths are often interrelated, but by addressing each separately we will see how they are distinct, how they overlap, and how blockbuster toys provided the right mix of qualities, at the right time, to transform the child.

Blockbuster toys also help *transform* parents. When a parent buys a toy that will help a child develop eye-hand coordination or learn the ABCs better than other toys can, the toy helps the parent in his or her endless quest to become an effective teacher. When a parent provides a plaything that inspires a child to emulate an important role model in that parent's view, it helps the parent become an effective guide. When the parent buys a toy that inspires a child to laugh, it helps the parent become an effective entertainer who delights in bringing a smile to a child's lips in a world where children are often expected to grow up too fast. The toys that best help parents wear the many hats they wish to wear have a greater chance of becoming blockbusters. They help the parents satisfy the many parental needs outlined in this chapter, including the need for a child's health, success, and happiness.

• *A blockbuster toy effectively communicates its transformation capability.* It has blockbuster marketing. This is achieved via a vast array of marketing venues, from advertising to promotion to packaging to public relations. When directed at children, blockbuster marketing helps them easily imagine what they could become, in reality or fantasy, if they owned the toy. When directed at parents, it helps them imagine how their children might be transformed by playing with the toy and thus how the parent will be transformed also. Hence, blockbuster marketing helps both child and parent witness the potential transformation. It demonstrates that, through use of the toy, they can get closer to their fantasies and realities than they could with a different toy. If the manufacturer's communications of these transformation qualities are superior to those of its competitors, it moves the toy further toward blockbuster status.

Our Goal

This book is designed to address these two central principles: the toy's ability to transform in fantasy or reality, and marketing's ability to accurately—and honestly—communicate the toy's transformation qualities. Blockbuster toys will be used as examples throughout the book to demonstrate these principles, while always relating back to core needs, features, play patterns, historical and societal context, and more.

The following chapters address the key blockbuster approaches that serve to transform children primarily, and the related ways they can transform parents. Those chapters are followed by ones that address the sundry marketing elements that strive to communicate this transformation in ways that will gain attention. The final chapter addresses the issue of responsibility, for if blockbuster toys transform children in blockbuster ways, great care must be taken to ensure that such a transformation be safe and in keeping with parents' desires (conflicting as those may be).

This is where the journey truly begins. We are about to better understand why some toys became blockbusters. The aim is to help the toymaker create the Next Big Thing that will ignite millions upon millions of smiles.

CHAPTER 3

Create a Master

Children come into a world with no apparent skills and must learn a multitude of tasks in order to survive, grow, and flourish. They quickly become aware that adults are the supreme masters in this world, and that children are the novices, always learning, failing, and striving. Because of this, children yearn to master many tasks, both large and small. Mastering a task helps children tell the world that they are advancing to the next level, that they are reaching important milestones, and that through diligence they can meet challenges. It helps children feel important in a world where they have so little control, a world in which they have been told for years when to rise in the morning, when to wash, when to eat, when to milk the cows (chores of any kind), when to study, and when to go to bed to begin the process again the next day.

Mastering a task helps children tell the world that they are special. It helps them feel competent in meeting challenges. And of course, it is very sweet when the task is one at which adults are not competent. That makes the child have some small degree of power over the adult world. Every parent experiences the moment when their child suddenly realizes that they can do something that the parent cannot. Victory over a parent is one of the greatest thrills for a child. When that occurs, the child's heart soars; long live the new master! That is the critical, timeless context in which mastery toys are born and excel.

In short, mastery builds self-esteem and ignites inner pride. These are core emotional needs that demand to be satisfied. Many of the very early toys—and many of today's toys—are about meeting simple challenges that build skills of some sort. They transform a child into an expert of something for the first time in the child's life. And when the child masters that simple challenge, it brings a smile to the child's lips.

This book will explore many types of mastery. But this chapter will focus upon the simplest and some of the most ancient of toys that have, in overt or subtle ways, allowed children become masters. The examples will demonstrate that a toy's ability to bring about seemingly trivial increases in a child's mastery can actually have an immense impact on its ability to become a blockbuster.

Create a Master of Simple Yet Challenging Tasks

Created thousands of years ago by a toymaker unknown to the world, the yo-yo was one of the first toys that provided a small skill for the child to master. For ages, children wrapped a thin string around their tiny fingers and let the disk fall, only to rise again, to the amazement of onlookers. To this very day, a child who masters the simple yo-yo feels like an expert, indeed. This small task is not about fun so much as it is about meeting a challenge. Becoming a master is the fun!

The modern history of the yo-yo really is a story of the Duncan brand. Donald Duncan was a businessman in California. He bought a yo-yo company founded in 1928 by Pedro Flores, who subsequently went to work for Duncan. It was Flores's new design that actually sparked a lot of interest. He did not tie the string to the axle but looped it around it instead. That allowed the yo-yo to spin in place ("sleep"). With that seemingly minor innovation, children could suddenly achieve far more advanced tricks such as "walk the dog." It greatly expanded the potential of the yo-yo. It heightened the toy's ability to be *on emotional target*, by allowing for far greater

Duncan yo-yos circa 1930s. Courtesy of collector Lucky J. Meisenheimer, M.D., with permission granted by Duncan.

mastery than ever before. The yo-yo craze expanded rapidly as more and more tricks were invented and mastered. These were not necessarily hard tricks, but they required time to perfect, which made them all the more worthy to master, which brought all the more recognition to those who could master them. The simple yo-yo, through a small innovation, suddenly presented larger tasks to be mastered, with greater creative potential. Says Steve Brown, U.S. National Yo-Yo Master and the marketing and promotions coordinator for Duncan Toys Company, "The timeless appeal of yo-yos can be attributed to two factors: the elegance of their simplicity, and the fact that they are just really, really cool. A yo-yo is basically just a wheel on a string. It is the creativity of generations that has made the yo-yo what it is today . . . a toy without limits."

Because it was so portable, the yo-yo became a pocket toy, making its way from home to home, neighborhood to neighborhood, highly visible and bearing witness to the child who mastered it. But such mastery could not be contained within the home or even the neighborhood. Yo-yo demonstrations were held, championships were created, and experts were proclaimed around the world. This type of highly visible, *playful marketing* did a lot to heighten public awareness and the credibility of the yo-yo. It identified the yo-yo as a prominent skill toy, one worth mastering. This effort, along with the simple innovation of the loop, helped this minor skill toy reach blockbuster status.

Duncan Toys expanded rapidly as a result, and by 1962 the company had sold some 45 million yo-yos to millions of would-be masters. In time, the company was purchased by another company. Competitors entered the picture. New technologies allowed the yo-yo to make sounds, glow in the dark, and even spin faster and faster. But at the heart of it, the yo-yo was always about mastering a simple task and then expanding upon it. The more tricks the child could perform, and perform flawlessly, the greater an expert they became. The child could go one step further by creating new tricks for others to emulate. That was grand.

Though through adult eyes the yo-yo looks as if it is about creating frivolous fun, it actually allows a child to achieve mastery in a world where they master so little else. Helping a child become a master of some small, visible, challenging, highly portable task can make for a blockbuster toy. It moved the yo-yo from simple plaything to serious skill, from everyday use to everyday enthusiam, from a flash in the pan to a piece of enduring culture. "The yo-yo is a true multigenerational toy," says Lucky J. Meisenheimer, M.D., author of *Lucky's Collector's Guide to 20th Century Yo-Yos*. "It is the only toy that has had repeat crazes affecting each generation of the 20th century."

Create a Master for Keeps

Archaeologists have found yet another blockbuster toy in every part of the world. It has appeared in 3,000-year-old tombs of Egyptian pharaohs. It has been found in digs of early Native American sites. Romans played with it, wrote about it, and were probably responsible for spreading it throughout the Old World. George Washington and Abraham Lincoln played with it. Daniel Defoe, author of *Robinson Crusoe*, included it in his stories. Some say that David killed Goliath with one. It has been made of clay, stone, flint, nuts, glass, and, of course . . . marble.

The game of marbles has various forms. Most common in the United States is a child kneeling, his thumb ready to launch a marble that is momentarily clutched within a bent forefinger that's touching the ground, his eyes squinting in concentration at an opponent's marble that he wishes to knock outside a perfectly drawn circle. It is the simplicity of competition that has allowed marbles to survive eons, one person against the next in a small test of skill and mastery. It was as portable and visible as the yo-yo, but the head-to-head competition ingrained in the play pulled two children together, making it a more social activity.

But some who played the game of marbles added one more dimension to it that helped make it a blockbuster toy. If you are playing *for keeps*, the victor obtains the spoils of the contest . . . the opponent's marble! Playing for keeps added a powerful wrinkle to the game. It put a child's plaything at risk (some parents hate this idea, I know). That motivated children (and adults who played) to practice as never before in order to prevent losing their prized marble to an opponent. Becoming a master was more important than ever. It placed the common game of marbles more *on emotional target* than ever before. There was considerable pride in victory, in the moment, and in the bag that contained all the marbles gained by competition. Marbles as a form of skill and mastery had taken a huge leap.

This simple idea of for keeps found its way into another, contemporary game and brand called Pokemon. In Pokemon, a competitor would collect "Pocket Monsters" and pit them against those of others for keeps. The greater the skill of the competitor, the greater the spoils they would obtain. Yes, many kids often play such games for fun and not for keeps. But for keeps is where the greatest excitement and challenges are piled up. A contest for keeps pumps adrenaline through our veins, young and old.

Create a Master of Endurance

A contemporary inventor, Arthur Melin, observed children in the South Pacific playing with bamboo hoops around their waists. The goal was to get the hoop spinning around the waist and, once that was achieved, see how long the spinning could be sustained. It was about skillful endurance. It was a form of fun that had been around for centuries and in many parts of the world, but no one ever thought to do anything with it. Intrigued by the sight, Melin's company, Wham-O, introduced the hoops into the United States in 1958 and sold some 25 million units, priced at $1.98 each. It was the Hula Hoop, a sensation that swept across the country and has made periodic resurgences as new generations discover this ancient toy.

So, how long can you keep it spinning? How many hoops can you spin at one time? The Hula Hoop represented a simple skill to be mastered. Once again, it was highly visible and portable. It was not so easy that the child would get bored with it, nor so difficult that they would become frustrated and drop the challenge. Very much like the yo-yo and marbles, it was just challenging

Hula Hoop poster circa 1965. Courtesy of Wham-O. © 2003 Wham-O, Inc. All rights reserved.

enough so that every child had the potential to become a master. And millions of children did. Never, ever underestimate the thrill of mastering a simple skill, particularly one that the novice has difficulty learning. Because once these skills are mastered, every child takes great pride in showing them off and teaching others.

A museum curator recently told me that in his travels, he sees many ancient children's games that are still played today in Third World countries but that have not yet made their way into the modern world. Perhaps no one thought to try. Blockbuster toys of old, because of their simple tasks to be mastered, have the potential to be blockbuster toys of today. The introduction of the Hula Hoop is a prime example. But many toymakers spend too much time trying to invent the future instead of trying to mine and reinvent the past.

Create a Master of Throw and Catch

The game of throw and catch has always been with us. It has been played with various instruments—often a ball—in every region of the world for thousands of years. There is something in this that is both subtle and grand. Most notably, perhaps, is the desire to become a master thrower and catcher. With such a designation comes the satisfaction of the aforementioned needs, among them pride, attention, and self-esteem. While this may sound frivolous, that basic concept has led to the creation of billion-dollar sports franchises including baseball, football, soccer, basketball, and many others. The mastery involved in the simple act of throwing and catching creates smiles, if only one can add a new twist to this ancient pastime.

One company took several unique approaches to the ancient activity of throw and catch and, in so doing, created a legacy. It was Wham-O. To begin, the company helped popularize an item as ubiquitous as the pie tin. But it was not just any pie tin. Some say it was similar to tins of the Frisbie Baking Company in Hartford, Connecticut. Yale students and townspeople had been tossing the company's pie tins since at least the 1920s. It is said that some would yell a warning of "Frisbie!" to passersbys who came within striking distance, much the same way that golfers yell, "Fore!" Others lay claim to the humble beginnings of the Frisbee as well, but Wham-O brought it to the attention of the world after a California building inspector, Fred Morrison, took a plastic version to the company. Wham-O bought the rights in 1955 and gave it the brand name of Frisbee in 1958.

The Frisbee was addicting, portable, and highly visible. But Wham-O added an important wrinkle. The company began to market the toy as a sport, and even introduced a professional version. That moment legitimized the Frisbee. It elevated the stature of all those who became Frisbee masters, thus increasing the pride associated with that title (*on emotional target*).

Frisbie pie tin from the Frisbie Baking Company, 1871-1958. From the author's personal collection.

Enthusiast groups formed, competitions followed, and experts were proclaimed (unleashing *playful marketing*). Being pronounced a true sport gave the Frisbee credibility and heightened the emotional rewards, even though most of the world casually played with it in backyards, front yards, public parks, and beaches. One more important element led the Frisbee to blockbuster status. It was introduced at a time that gave it immense context. It became linked to the hippie movement of the sixties, forever associated with being young (*on trend*). Though there were undoubtedly other toys that the sixties youth movement could have adopted while protesting the war or listening to concerts, it was the Frisbee that was serendipitously adopted (*X Factor*), perhaps because the company also did a great job of demonstrating the product at youth hangouts (more *playful marketing*). To this day, to play with a Frisbee is to be youthful. Legitimized by being positioned as a true sport and connected to the youth movement of that day, the Frisbee went from being an everyday pie tin to being a blockbuster toy. It was *on emotional target* and *on trend*.

Wham-O was not done. It decided to take another swing at the very simple concept of throw and catch. This time, however, it created a ball out of synthetic rubber. The ball was supercharged, compressed under a thousand pounds of pressure per square inch. When dropped, the ball bounced back to nearly where it had been dropped from, giving it a resiliency of over 90 percent. If hurled at the ground, the ball could bounce over a house, down the street, around the corner, and far out of sight. It wasn't all that easy to catch, but it was sure fun to throw, which was part of the charm and the mastery. It was the Superball brand and the year was 1965. It was for demonstrating just how high you could bounce the ball and how chaotic the outcome might be. The company soon thereafter introduced mini, golf, and baseball versions, all with a notable bounce that seemed to defy gravity and land wherever it pleased. The Superball was an ancient toy made new again.

Wham-O has a knack for transforming and transporting kids and adults alike. Peter Sgromo, marketing director at Wham-O, says:

> The world is more chaotic than it has ever been before and the Baby Boom is transporting itself back to a gentler time when life was simpler. The Slip'N Slide®, Frisbee®, and Hula Hoop® brands are catalysts to transport them back to their childhood. And they are bringing their own children along for the ride. These brands are like comfort food. They represent calmness, tranquility, and simplicity. They bring back the joy they felt as a child. People are transformed to become part of the actual toy. This is because Slip'N Slide, Frisbee, and Hula Hoop are basic and appeal to basic fundamental human nature. The most important moving part of a Wham-O toy is the person playing with it. They are designed to make people work their bodies and minds. Frisbee transforms one into the fascination of flight. The supple body movement makes a child an integral part of a shooping Hula Hoop. And Slip'N Slide appeals to our innate nature to dive. It is fascinating to put these toys in a backyard in front of a group of children who have never seen them before. It becomes automatic and human nature to swing a Hula Hoop on the hip, to throw a Frisbee into the air, or to slide belly first on a Slip'N Slide.

A different company took an alternative approach to the art of throw and catch. They didn't create a hard resilient ball, but a soft foamy one . . . the Nerf Ball. Introduced in 1969, it had the opposite properties. This was the gentle ball, the one that could be played with in the home because it was furniture friendly. It became the safe, anytime, anyplace ball. You couldn't break a window or aquarium even if you wanted too. It allowed children to take one of their favorite mastery, skill toys indoors, where the other, harder skill toys were not allowed! Over 4 million Nerf Balls were sold by the end of the first year. Nerf expanded into footballs and shooting activities like Nerf Blaster and Nerf Bow & Arrow, which allowed Nerf to connect with many different emotional needs, thus becoming a line-extension success story as well.

The simple act of throwing and catching has fascinated children and adults for thousands of years and, with various twists, has created the opportunity to turn common children into uncommon masters.

Create an Intellectual Master

Perhaps the greatest thrill for many of us is to excel in mental feats, to prove that we are smarter than another. This is perhaps even more important for children, because of their novice position in life. So anytime a child can master a game that demonstrates intellectual prowess, it is thrilling indeed.

A game very similar to checkers was found in excavations of the city of Ur in a country that is known today as Iraq. Archaeologists place the date of the game at 3000 B.C. Puzzles are also ancient and have a similar impact upon us. They test a child's (and adult's) ability to find solutions and order in a world filled with disorder. In the modern era, a lecturer at the Academy of Applied Arts and Crafts in Budapest intuitively knew this. He took a rare interest in geometry, construction, and combination theory and used his knowledge to create a novel toy. It is a three-by-three-by-three color-coded cube that can rotate on any axis. Each of the cube's six sides has nine squares. Before they are altered, each side has a different color (with each of the nine squares sharing that same color). When the cube is twisted back and forth, the colors are mixed on each side. The object of the puzzle is to match the squares so that each side is all one color again.

The inventor was Erno Rubik, and this was the Rubik's Cube® puzzle. It's a complex toy with a simple, habit-forming objective. Erno's students became obsessed with it. Once you tried to "fix" the puzzle, it was difficult to put it down until you got it right. But it was hard to get it right! The first manufactured cubes were introduced in Budapest in 1977. They

The Rubik's Cube. From the author's personal collection. Use of the Rubik's Cube® is by permission of Seven Towns Ltd. www.rubiks.com.

reached major toy fairs around the world in 1980 and found their way into millions of homes soon thereafter. In an interesting way, the Rubik's Cube shared the same qualities with the yo-yo and Hula Hoop: it was a simple idea, highly visible, and highly portable. People were greatly motivated to pick it up and try it. They shared it with friends. They didn't have to learn the rules of chess. They simply had to spin it around and begin. Its simplicity immediately engaged people, but its complexity of solution captured them. *How can something that looks so simple be so complex?* That was the beauty of the Rubik's Cube and the element that put it squarely *on emotional target*. It enticed people to become instant masters, but then the solution proved far more challenging and elusive than they thought. They got stuck like flies on flypaper. Their intellect would refuse to accept defeat by something that looked so simple, and so they continued to play with it. Apparent simplicity, mixed with actual complexity, made it a blockbuster toy.

Children and adults alike sought help on how to master it. Over sixty books were published to help those who were . . . well . . . Rubikly challenged. The Rubik's Cube brought pride to those who could master it and envy to the millions who could not. It sold over 100 million units. This simple toy spawned enthusiasts, exhibitions, competitions, and champions, all hallmarks of the effective, *playful marketing* of mastery toys. Rubik soon introduced related puzzles such as Rubik's Pocket Cube (two by two by two), Rubik's Revenge (four by four by four), Rubik's Triamid, and others. All had the same object—to challenge every child (and adult) to become a master.

Create an Educational Master

The earliest of toys were often crafted by parents with a dual purpose: to inspire a child to smile and to provide an opportunity to learn and develop. Many contemporary toys strive for this objective, too. One of these toys was introduced in 1965 using the same basic technology as Thomas Edison's gramophone. Its simple purpose was to help very young children learn words and associate them with common barnyard animals. When the child moved the arrow on the circular toy toward the picture of an animal, say a cow, and then pulled the string, the toy would respond, "The cow says moo!" It was the See 'n Say, The Farmer Says. The toy was rather innovative, but it also was introduced at a time that gave it great context. Since most kids in the sixties were not living on the farm but had moved to the suburbs, it brought the sights and sounds of the farm to city kids everywhere. Parents were able to give their

See 'n Say, The Farmer Says. Courtesy of
Fisher-Price.

children an educational experience not only about words but
also about a lifestyle that was rapidly fading away . . . the family
farm. In that context, See 'n Say was squarely *on trend* by connecting itself with the parents' longing for another time, a nostalgic time. See 'n Say has varied its theme over the years in
order to be *regenerative* and has tackled many other learning
elements, but its simplicity, its focus on helping a child learn a
simple task, and importantly the context in which it was introduced made it a blockbuster toy.

Many toymakers have dabbled in the education market to
help children master developmental skills. Among them is one
of the first true blockbusters in this arena, Fisher-Price. The
company has taken great care over the years to develop a wide
variety of toys that help children grow and hence become masters of their worlds. It has done an amazingly beneficial job of
being *on emotional target* for the child and parent alike. Its stated
mission is to "support today's families with young children

through a breadth of products and services that make early childhood more fun and enriching." It has created toys to help a child develop motor skills, improve eye-hand coordination, learn the alphabet, recognize animals and objects, learn cause and effect, and more. Fisher-Price has been in existence since the 1930s and has undoubtedly helped millions of children develop and master their worlds.

Craig Spitzer, vice-president of marketing research for Fisher-Price, says:

> Young children live in a world with many restrictions. Their visual references are often kneecaps and hubcaps—the perspective you see in "Rugrats" cartoons. The word they hear most often is "Don't." "Don't put that in your mouth!" "Don't put your finger in that socket!" "Don't touch that!" Fisher-Price toys help children get a good start in life by empowering them beyond their limited visual and social horizons. First, there are simpler toys that facilitate simple skill mastery. These provide children with the joy of cleverly designed feedback to their actions, which provides a sense of pride when they learn how to cause the effects. Then, Fisher-Price offers more complex toys that allow children to use the skills they have learned, layering imaginative stories into the play. With these toys, children explore their imaginations, becoming actors in the drama around them. For example, when a child learns to push the Corn Popper, she gets that wonderful visual and auditory ball play. Now she is ready to take that skill and push a play vacuum, imagining she is Mommy or Daddy doing chores around the house. She learns that pushing buttons can be fun, because that causes the "Sesame Street" characters to pop up in the Poppin' Pals toy. Then she takes the "button-pushing cause-effects" skill to the Elmo's Cell Phone and gets cause-effect, button-pushing play, plus the fantasy that she has cell-phone conversations, like the adults around her. A boy's first Little People toy is usually a small one, like the Fire Truck. At first, the fun of the toy is just finding all the ways he can activate its lights, sounds, and phrases. After he knows how to "work" toys

like this, he is ready for the classic Fisher-Price Little People Barn. Now, in addition to just activating sound and lights, when he puts the chicken in the nest, he gets the clucking sound and can enact stories with the toy: "OK, animals, it is time to go to bed . . . everyone into the barn."

The care Fisher-Price has taken to help young children become early masters of their worlds is significant because the company has reached the perfect blend of transforming the child into a greater master while helping the parents in their efforts to become helpful guides.

Leapfrog Enterprises Inc. entered this arena in 1995 with a modest $3 million in sales, and by the end of 2002, annual sales rose to nearly $532 million, stemming from a variety of innovative, technology-based educational products that help children develop their intellectual prowess. The brand is becoming a blockbuster because the products achieve the right blend of education and interactivity, with great sensitivity to and understanding of the age and stage of childhood development. The products teach and engage a wide variety of children in such subjects as reading, math, science, music, geography, and social studies.

The Walt Disney Company has been involved with the development of toys for a long while and is always seeking to find those arenas where they can leverage their storytelling expertise to help children learn and develop. In so doing, Disney has several blockbuster educational brands in the making. Jennifer Anopolsky, vice-president of corporate brand management at The Walt Disney Company, says:

> Consumers have become much more savvy than when Disney licensed its first toy. Today, parents are looking for toys that not only engage their children but also nurture their development. At The Walt Disney Company, this has led to a focus on early childhood development and a specific subbrand, Playhouse Disney, for preschool learning. Under this banner, Disney is

creating new characters, content, and activities designed to help preschool children learn and grow. Likewise, this focus led to the acquisition of The Baby Einstein Company and a commitment to creating developmental products for the youngest children and their parents.

With companies like Fisher-Price and The Walt Disney Company giving attention to a child's need to become a master, the future looks bright for children.

Mastery Everywhere

There are other mastery toys worth noting, like the Pogo Stick, Jump Rope, and Jacks. Forms of these toys have existed for centuries, but new wrinkles renewed them for new generations. Jacks are based upon many ancient counting games. The object of Jacks is quite simple: throw a ball into the air and scoop up as many Jacks as you possibly can before the ball drops. It's an extremely simple task that inspires mastery, which is why the toy is one of the most widespread in the world. The master of Jacks is the child who can speed right through the easy twosies and threesies and right to the tensies. Jump Rope dates back to Dutch settlers in America during the seventeenth century. But girls gave it immense context by making it a highly social activity. Girls also moved it into a form of pop culture by inventing rhymes and inserting songs to reflect the times in which they lived, allowing Jump Rope to be perpetually *on trend*. Yet once again, simple mastery was important, and to this day both boys and girls strive to increase their Jump Rope skills. National Jump Rope organizations have formed, and competitions have been deemed worthy of coverage on ESPN.

More complex forms of mastery will be explored in other chapters. But they all have the same foundation: an apparently simple challenge that begs the child to conquer it. Those toys that smashed the barrier between mere playthings and blockbuster toys often did so because they *transformed* the child into a master better than other options could. They often introduced an innovation that expanded the mastery potential (*on emotional target*) such as the Duncan yo-yo (innovation allowed for greater mastery), Frisbee (professional version legitimized it as a sport), marbles and Pokemon (*for keeps* increased the stakes), and Rubik's Cube (making the complex look simple). Several of the above brands are also good examples of those that were invented *on trend,* including See 'n Say (nostalgia of the farm) and Frisbee (sixties youth movement). Most of these mastery blockbusters also benefited from *playful marketing* that inspired enthusiasts to meet and compete on both a neighborhood and world stage. All of the above brands have updated themselves with newer versions and innovations that allowed them to stay current (*regenerative*).

The Next Big Thing: Basic Principles

• Invent toys and games that help a child best satisfy the need to become *a master,* thus being *on emotional target.* Even small increases in mastery can have massive results.

• Look to the past for great toys and ideas, and then add a touch of innovation to help the child attain even greater mastery.

• Uncover a simple, playful task that is *easy* to repeat but *hard* to master. The playful task should require practice and learning to meet the challenge. It should be highly visible and portable, which inspires group interest, participation, word of mouth, pride, and "showing off."

• Make it a serious sport. Inspire enthusiasts. Help them congregate, communicate, and compete. Honor the champions and the nonchampions. They deserve it.

CHAPTER 4

Create a Creator

Children were born to create, stretch their minds, and allow youthful imaginations to soar. The desire to create is as old as mankind and might be even more woven into the fabric of our existence than we know. Noted motivational speaker and author Tom Morris takes a brave guess at the very meaning of life. He believes it is connected to what he calls Loving Creativity. He defines it as "the creative building of new structures, new relationships, new solutions, and new possibilities for our world."

One must admit that the very act of creation is at the core of our beings. Humankind is on an endless quest to create—we create children, homes, products, art, music, dance, theories, technology, recipes, and so on. Now that scientists have mapped the DNA chain, we are coming closer to creating and altering life at its most fundamental level.

We create. And we recreate. Perhaps it is our innate desire to fashion a world more to our liking, to strive toward perfection, to experiment with new possibilities, or to achieve mastery over our environment, all perhaps to satisfy the core emotional needs of pride and accomplishment. Regardless of the reason, more than any other endeavor, we create. And there is no better expression of this than that exhibited by our children. They wish desperately to create, and thus transform themselves into creators. When toys help them achieve creator status in a grand way, they become blockbusters. Many of these blockbusters took different paths to achieve that status, wherein lie the learning and the opportunities.

Create Artists

An exuberant four-year-old Katie dashes to her mother. The child is holding a beautifully drawn picture she labored long to perfect. It contains a green, box-shaped house with squiggly walls and a brown chimney with black smoke billowing into a scribbled blue sky. Birds fly around the plume of smoke, just like the ones Katie saw yesterday. In the front yard of her illustrated home are an ultragreen lawn and a garden filled with sunflowers almost as tall as the house. The home has a window with four huge panes of glass. Within each pane, Katie has drawn a different family member—her mom with blonde hair, her balding dad with his three remaining hairs sticking up straight, her teenage brother with dyed red hair, and beautiful little Katie herself. This is Katie's world. This is also perfection, as Katie knows it. She has recreated this perfection with brilliantly colored scribbles.

"Mommy!" Katie shouts as she rushes into her mother's embrace and is lifted high. "Look what I drew!" Katie beams.

Mom looks at the drawing and smiles wide. "It's beautiful!" she says as she gives Katie a loving hug. "And I know just the perfect place for it." With Katie still in her arms, Mom moves to the refrigerator and proudly sticks Katie's drawing on the door with a refrigerator magnet. "Wait until Dad sees that!" Mom says, as she once again gives Katie a hug.

This moment is timeless. It has been reenacted millions and millions of times around the world, by millions upon millions of fathers and mothers with their daughters and sons. This is no small thing. Though it takes only a moment to occur, it is wrapped in an enduring and powerful set of emotions such as pride, love, and joy. Children have an intense desire to create and be recognized for their creations. Parents love to help their children unleash their creative potential. Helping children transform into creators, then, also helps parents become skillful guides.

Many products and brands help give birth to the moment described above, but foremost among them is the Crayola brand of crayons. The brand has inspired a multitude of children to create worlds reflecting their own as well as worlds that go beyond. It all began in 1885 when two cousins named Edwin Binney and C. Harold Smith established a chemical company that manufactured red pigments for painting barns, along with slate pencils, chalk, shoe polish, and printing ink. In time, they came up with the idea of converting the colored sticks they used to mark boxes in the factory for the educational market. Crayola Crayons were born in 1903, the name being derived from two French words meaning "oily chalk." The first box contained only eight colors (orange, yellow, black, brown, green, red, blue, and purple), but it placed the Crayola brand squarely *on emotional target* by providing easy-to-use colorful instruments that expanded children's ability to be *transformed* into skilled artists and creators. This is an eternally strong emotional need that was all but ignored in 1903—wherein lived the immense opportunity!

By 1993, Crayola Crayons were offered in a box featuring ninety-six colors, which represented only a fraction of over six hundred colors that Crayola has produced over the years. They have come in variations such as fluorescent, glittery, and even color-change and scented crayons to engage the child's other senses. This expanded the creator's ability for self-expression. By reinventing itself to reflect the fashions of the day, the Crayola brand has helped itself stay *on trend* and be *regenerative.* Today, over 3 billion Crayola Crayons are sold each year in over eighty countries. Binney & Smith have sold more than 120 billion crayons since 1903. That is enough, says the company, to circle the world over two hundred times. According to a Yale University study, the scent of Crayola Crayons is among the

Crayola Crayons, 1903. Courtesy of Binney & Smith. Crayola, chevron, and serpentine designs are registered trademarks; smile design is a trademark of Binney & Smith Inc.; used with permission.

twenty most recognizable to American adults. Just imagine
how many moments like Katie's they have helped create, and
how many Katies they helped turn into creators. One advertisement proclaims that Crayola is "Putting Creativity Back into
Kids' Hands." The brand's march to help kids become creators
is inspiring, and it demands creativity on the part of the company, too. "It's amazing where a box of eight crayons and a lot
of creativity has taken us," says the president and chief executive officer of Binney & Smith, Mark Schwab. "We see a very
bright future ahead."

Create a blank slate—a blank canvas—for the child, and you
have the potential to turn that child into an artist. Arthur
Granjean knew this, too. He introduced his new invention at
the 1959 International Toy Fair in Nuremberg, Germany. Like
Crayola Crayons, the invention allowed a child to create something from nothing. The difference was that Granjean's invention provided a unique and innovative drawing surface and
knobs that children would control to create anything their
hearts desired. With a few shakes, the slate became blank
again, adding to the delight and to re-creation. It was the Etch
A Sketch brand. It added a touch of innovation to something
old, a blank slate. It connected with the rise of mechanical contraptions, making it perfectly *on trend.* Other versions have
been introduced over the years to create a contemporary feel
and to be *regenerative,* such as the Zooper Sounds Etch A
Sketch, with sound effects, the Travel Etch A Sketch, which is
a miniature version, and a CD-ROM. But the emotional connection stays the same, providing children with a simple tool to
reproduce the world around them and improve upon it. With
an Etch A Sketch in hand, the child is a creator and artist.

In 1965, inventor Denys Fisher went a different way. While
he, too, provided a blank slate for the child to create upon, he
used the form and function of geometry, much as when Erno
Rubik created the Rubik's Cube brand. But Fisher used the
insights to turn children into modern artists. He created the

Spirograph Design Toy, those plastic circles and gears that cause brightly colored pens to whirl about, thus creating intricate designs. Suddenly, the child could create astonishing illustrations never before imagined. "Look what I did!" was given new meaning, because a child never imagined that their tiny hands could give birth to such complex and arresting designs. The Spirograph transformed children from creative scribblers into creative masters and elevated refrigerator doors from handy creations to modern-art galleries. It allowed children to reach the perfection of form and, as a result, attain perfection as contemporary artists.

One brand helped children reach creator status not just as illustrators but sculptors, allowing them to express themselves in a new form. Enter Play-Doh Modeling Compound, a brand that children have used since 1956 to give shape to their ideas and to become sculptors no less than Michelangelo (at least in their minds' eyes). Suddenly, children could create in three dimensions. They could make wizards and dragons, moms and dads, pets and wild beasts, statues and butterflies. While the initial Play-Doh was off-white, it soon was available in multiple colors and glow-in-the-dark versions, and it was eventually packed with various "factories" that helped children manufacture more true-to-life creations, ranging from ice-cream stores to beauty shops. The brand proved to be highly *regenerative* in this way by giving children contemporary methods to both replicate their world and build upon it in three-dimensional form. Play-Doh turned children from scribblers into sculptors, thus fulfilling a strong emotional need that had been ignored, placing it well *on emotional target.* It connected with the same passion borne by Michelangelo, who stared at a slab of rock and wondered, What if? Approximately 95 million cans of Play-Doh compound are manufactured each year, with 2 billion cans sold since 1956 across more than seventy-five countries. That's a pretty good legacy for a brand that was derived from a wallpaper cleaner.

Another brand that helped children become creators and artists of sorts began with James Wright, an engineer working for General Electric in 1943. Looking to create a synthetic rubber compound to aid the war effort, he combined boric acid and silicone oil in a test tube. It polymerized into a gooey substance. Wright removed it from the test tube, examined it, and then, in a moment of pure serendipity, tossed it onto the floor. The puttylike substance bounced. But it wasn't until 1949 that anyone tried to make it into a plaything. That occurred when an owner of a toy store and a marketer by the name of Peter Hodgson decided to advertise it as such in a catalog. This is an early example of how *playful marketing* helped turn an oddity into a toy. The new brand outsold everything in the catalog, except Crayola Crayons. A year later, and with a new name, the blockbuster toy brand was born . . . Silly Putty. The creative use of the Silly Putty brand is entirely in the hands of its users. While lifting images from newsprint, typically comics, is the favorite use, Binney & Smith have cataloged a vast array of other uses, including cleaning computer keyboards, plugging leaks, removing lint from clothing, and leveling the leg of a wobbly table, not to forget simply squeezing it, stretching it like a rubber band, or bouncing it around a room. To celebrate the brand's fiftieth anniversary, Binney & Smith tied into the brand's amazing ability to inspire consumers to invent new uses. It staged a contest to find the "most silly, most inventive and even most practical uses for the pliable plaything." Since 1950, more than 300 million Silly Putty eggs have been sold.

Create Inventors

Some brands transform children not just into skilled creators and artists but inventors. Charles Pajeau created the Tinkertoy brand in 1913. With wooden spools with eight holes around the circumference of each, and a larger hole in the middle, Tinkertoy could be connected by wooden sticks to achieve a multitude of creations and configurations. It allowed

Silly Putty. Courtesy of Binney & Smith. Silly Putty is a registered trademark of Binney & Smith Inc.

a child to become a "tinker," a noble form of creator whose aim is to create such contraptions as bridges, windmills, and airplanes. This activity was *on trend* because it came at a time when the industrial world was continuing to expand and children could readily see adult contraptions of all sorts take form. A multitude of tiny children's fingers ached to build the same things, and the Tinkertoy brand allowed them to achieve it.

Created in 1916 and finally introduced to the public in 1924, Lincoln Logs allow millions of children to feel the thrill of creating their own cabins. They transform children into a different form of creators and inventors: architects. With Lincoln Logs, children could suddenly create true-to-life homesteads and forts that were born out of their imaginations or carefully guided by Lincoln Log designs. Lincoln Logs, in effect, became an instructor in rudimentary architecture, allowing children to use logs notched at each end to create sturdy homes with doors, windows, chimneys, and roofs. Then children could "live" in the world of their creation, using both imagination and miniature figures to bring their home, their town, their society to life. Lincoln Logs brought out the architect within the child. It's not so ironic that Lincoln Logs were created by John Lloyd Wright, the son of famous architect Frank Lloyd Wright. Since these cabins, made of logs, looked like the one Pres. Abraham Lincoln grew up in, they were given his name. That decision was significant, because it allowed the brand to link to America's own proud past, connecting it with another emotional driver, patriotism. Lincoln Logs was *on trend* for this and more. It was created at a time when the populace continued to move to cities yet still had a nostalgic connection to a simpler past. That connection undoubtedly remains to this very day. Over 100 million Lincoln Log sets have been sold to parents for the amusement of their young architects.

A. C. Gilbert was born in 1884 and graduated from Yale Medical School in 1909. But his heart was not in it. He wanted to make toys. One day while noting workmen riveting steel beams to create an electric railway, he wondered what it would be like to allow a child to do the same, to feel like a true architect and construction worker rolled into one, with all the right tools of the industrialized world: metal beams, bolts, screws, gears, pulleys, and even motors. Gilbert's vision led to the invention of the Erector Set. With it, children created true-to-life construction and machines that reflected the period. Building skyscrapers and machines was suddenly within a child's reach. "Look what I did!" suddenly had greater form

Erector Set circa 1960. From the author's personal collection. With approval of Meccano (outside the U.S., Erector Set is sold under the name of Meccano).

and meaning. Children were building not just homesteads and townships, but trucks and amusement rides and, in effect, an industrial world in motion. It moved children closer to being real builders of items they saw in the world. The Erector Set uniquely *transformed* children from architects into near-real industrialists. The brand was uniquely *on trend* and *on emotional target*. Worried in 1918 when the Council of National Defense proposed a ban on all toy sales to aid the World War I effort, Gilbert pleaded with the council that toys were "blueprints of future men and women who would fight wars and preserve the peace." He went on to plead that by depriving youngsters of toys, especially educational toys, the nation would lose a generation of doctors, engineers, and scientists. Gilbert understood that toys were not just playthings, as they have the power to transform children into responsible adults. The council was persuaded by the argument, and the proposed ban on toy sales was withdrawn.

Enter Ole Kirk Christiansen. A carpenter by trade, he made wooden products, including toys, during the Great Depression. Later focusing on toys, he named his company LEGO, meaning "play well." During the 1940s he saw the need for an easy-to-use construction set, one that used studs on top of each brick and hollows on the bottom. It allowed the bricks to snap easily together. Using the new form of plastic-injection molding in 1947, his team eventually created simple *plastic* bricks. His innovation was first named Automatic Binding Bricks in 1949, but the brand eventually became known as LEGO bricks. The LEGO brand benefits from all of the insights that came before: the child as creator, playing the role of artist, inventor, architect, and industrialist. But the LEGO Company used the new medium of plastic, thus putting it *on trend*. And beyond supplying building bricks alone, LEGO began to add an assortment of designs, vehicles, characters, and themes (e.g., underwater, jungle, space, and knighthood). These allowed children over the years to not only build structures, but to build adventures as well, thus connecting with a variety of emotional needs, which has helped the brand be *regenerative* year after year. It's been estimated that the LEGO Company has created over 300 billion LEGO bricks.

Create the Ultimate Creators

The ultimate step toward creation is to create some form of life itself, if only a semblance thereof. The Mr. Potato Head brand seems like an unlikely candidate for such an amazing endeavor, yet it is. In 1952, George Lerner designed a set of plastic face pieces that would allow a child to turn an ordinary potato, as well as other vegetables and fruits, into a person with eyes, ears, a nose, and a mouth. It gave a personality to an otherwise nonliving object. Kids were given the chance to create people. It would be another eight years before the toy actually came with a plastic potato body, thus eliminating the need for the parent to supply the potato. But Mr. Potato Head was the tip of an iceberg.

Then came the Thingmaker sets, a toy brand that brought children even closer to the feeling of becoming grand creators. Introduced in 1964 with Creepy Crawlers, Thingmaker allowed children to create snakes, bugs, bats, and more in various shapes, colors, and gruesomeness. Children did so by filling metal molds with colorful plastic goop, which, when heated in a toylike oven and cooled, hardened into a flexible, rubbery creature. Kids were not only creators, but now *transformed* into mad scientists. Mattel followed upon the success of Creepy Crawlers with other molds that produced Fighting Men, Creeple People, and more. But at the bottom of many of these creations was the notion that children could become their own version of young Dr. Frankenstein. It was transforming.

But one toy brought this life-giving ability to the ultimate end, that of creating real life, a truly amazing miracle. Harold von Braunhut had a simple vision: to let children touch the thrill of being true creators. He developed a kit in 1960 comprised of the essentials—an aquarium and brine-shrimp eggs. Add water to the aquarium, fill it with the shrimp eggs in a latent state, and in time they hatch. Feed them with the nutrients provided, and life begins to swim its way around its new home. The child, *transformed* into life's creator, could now watch in utter amazement, full of pride and awe that he had a hand in its creation. As the babies matured, they looked a bit like monkeys, noted von Braunhut. So the toy brand that was first called Instant Life became known as the Sea Monkeys brand. It allowed children to truly experience what it is like to have a hand in creating life.

Imagine that from a mere toy! And so the circle completes. Parents beget children, who are born with an intense desire to create, who in time become creators themselves. Maybe Tom Morris was right all along. The very purpose of life is to create.

Creation Everywhere

There are many other toys that have satisfied the child's need to create, from chemistry sets to jewelry makers. They each have the ability to transform children into various personas or professions, just as other toys transform children into artists (Crayola), or sculptors (Play-Doh), or general inventors (Tinkertoy), or architects (Lincoln Logs), or industrialists (Erector Sets), or mad scientists (Creepy Crawlers), or even actual life-givers (Sea Monkeys). Throughout this book we will continue to touch upon a child's intense desire to be transformed into a creator of one sort or another. New toys that can do this in ways reflecting our contemporary world will be highly *on trend*.

The Next Big Thing: Basic Principles

• Invent toys that help children transform into grand *creators* in ways that are more real than previously possible: the artist, the sculptor, the inventor, the industrialist, the life-giver, and more.

• Look to an adult's world and their creators in art, science, and industry so as to create a toy brand that will allow children to mimic the same. Discover the kind of creators whom children want to emulate today. Look to the newest forms and design possibilities. These will put your toy *on trend.*

• Add a "construction/creating" element to the products you already offer. Allow children to build all or part of them. All toy brands can benefit from this, for when children are even partially responsible for the creation of their playthings, they feel greater ownership of them.

CHAPTER 5

Create a Nurturer

The power of creation lies in the intense desire for self-expression. But once the creation begins to manifest, our ingrained nurturing instinct pulls at that part of us that yearns to take care of our creation, to help it grow and to be successful (in fantasy or actuality). Just as adults have this strong emotional need, so do our children.

For young girls, this can be a prelude to motherhood. Toys are one way that girls can choose to emulate their own mothers and to practice the basics of nurturing before the day arrives for real. In ancient times, and in many parts of the world to this day, baby dolls served a profound purpose, to train a girl to be a mother. Such dolls, dating back thousands of years, have been found in archaeological digs of all cultures, and they remain an enduring part of the toy box. The absolute pervasiveness of baby dolls is strong testimony to girls' immense need to give sustenance to others. Boys express this need in subtler but still powerful ways. They care for their pet dogs, hamsters, guinea pigs, and snakes. Toys that have addressed a boy's need to nurture, but in a boy-accepting way, have flourished.

Many toys in contemporary times have tried to transform children into nurturers by enticing that part of children's personas to come out and play. Yet only a handful of these toys offered uniquely motivating features and cues that led to intimate play patterns, allowing them to become truly blockbuster toys.

Sometimes it requires a bit of luck, for sure. But more importantly, it requires that the toymaker realize that he is not making an "inanimate" toy and not selling just an "expressionless" plaything. He is carefully *crafting a persona* for the toy, one that is in dire need of being loved, protected, and nurtured. The toy's neediness is the key element that ignites young hearts and transforms everyday children into caring nurturers and everyday toys into uncommon blockbuster toys.

Saving Bears

One blockbuster toy had an atypical beginning in November of 1902. A group of avid hunters went bear hunting in the wilds of Mississippi. Just to be absolutely clear, they were there to kill bears, eat them, stuff them, and probably mount their heads on some wall in grand testimony to the hunter's prowess. Some members of the party spotted an adult bear, tracked it, set the hunting dogs after it, exhausted it, and finally cornered the animal near a water hole, where they were about to shoot it. According to one account, the trapped bear fought back and killed a hunting dog before it, too, was severely wounded by the dogs (one of several story variations claims that the bear was actually singed by a forest fire, and that's how hunters found it). In any case, the hunters who had descended upon the bear paused and then called for the celebrity guest of the hunting party to come to the front. That man was Theodore Roosevelt, twenty-sixth president of the United States. Upon finding the wounded bear cornered, exhausted, and tied to a tree by other hunters in the party, the president was given the chance to shoot it, thus affording him the honor of the kill. The leaders of the hunting party wanted to be sure that the president got what he came for, to kill his bear. But after seeing the bear in such a sorry state, the president refused, stating it was unsportsmanlike to shoot a trapped animal. According to this account, the bear was eventually shot anyway, not for sport but to put the poor creature out of its misery.

But that was not the way the story was eventually told to the world. In the version of the story that is considered slightly fabricated (several versions are everywhere making it hard to discern the truth), the bear was not an adult bear but a small and frightened bear cub. This version of the story goes on to say that when President Roosevelt was given the chance to shoot it, he spared its life. It lived! That was the tale that spread around the world like wildfire, thanks to a newspaper cartoonist named Clifford Berryman who worked for the *Washington Post*. He depicted "Teddy's bear" in several cartoons. They cast the

1902 cartoon, "Drawing the Line in Mississippi," by Clifford Berryman. Courtesy of the *Washington Post* and the National Museum of American History, Smithsonian Institution, Behring Center. Reprinted with permission.

president as a man who protected a child-cub in dire need. It was a noble, though many say false, story of a helpless baby animal and the man who saved it. That's the story that ignited the passion of the world. Interestingly, the cartoonist was using the tale not only to reflect the president's stance on saving the bear but to make political commentary on the president's other task for the trip, that of settling a border dispute between Mississippi and Louisiana. The original cartoon was entitled, "Drawing the Line in Mississippi."

Morris Michtom saw an opportunity in this precious moment. He asked his wife to stitch together plush toys in the shape of a bear cub. They sent one of the bears to the president and asked permission to name it after him. The president replied, "Dear Mr. Michtom, I don't think my name is likely to be worth much in the toy bear business, but you are welcome to use it." The Teddy Bear was born, named after Teddy Roosevelt. It went on sale in the Michtoms' novelty store in Brooklyn, New York, in 1903.

Though the Teddy Bear has sold millions, it's helpful to remember that this blockbuster toy was not simply a cute bear. Its thrust to blockbuster status needs to be put into the proper context of the moment of its inception. It depicted a frightened bear cub that desperately needed help. Millions of children wanted to protect that bear cub, too. That put it *on emotional target*. The bear cub was linked to an immensely popular international figure whose star was still rising. That put it *on trend*. That's what made the Teddy Bear a success. Today, the Teddy Bear continues to sell quite well out of inertia and nostalgia, though the story that catapulted it into the blockbuster stratosphere has faded. It also helped its inventor, Morris Michtom, found the Ideal Toy Company, which became one of the largest in the United States. Unfortunately for Mr. Michtom, he never trademarked his creation, so many other toymakers soon followed with their versions of "Teddy's bear."

Original Teddy Bear, 1903. Courtesy of the National Museum of American History, Smithsonian Institution, Behring Center.

Adopting Babies

Let's fast forward to 1977. A twenty-two-year-old art-school student named Xavier Roberts designed a line of dolls called "Little People" that were absolutely adorable and "adoptable." To pay his tuition, he sold the dolls at arts and crafts shows to parents willing to pay a forty-dollar "adoption" fee. In 1982, "Little People" were renamed Cabbage Patch Kids, and the toy world was about to change. The Cabbage Patch Kids brand was one of the first true blockbuster toys of the 1980s. Sudden demand for the playthings created an unexpected shortage, keeping many parents waiting in long lines during the 1983 holiday season. It's important to note that Cabbage Patch Kids were introduced into a world filled with mechanical dolls that would eat and move and such. Cabbage Patch Kids had no such mechanical feature, yet at the peak of its success in 1985, sales of the dolls were reported at $600 million. By 1991, over 70 million Cabbage Patch Kids had been adopted. It astonished the industry.

One might ask, why did this doll achieve blockbuster status and not the thousands of other baby dolls that had come before it . . . or since? It was because Cabbage Patch Kids had all the right cues. The initial quality of the dolls was superb, with quilted and handmade detail. It gave a lifelike quality to the doll. But more importantly, it was positioned as a parentless baby in need. Children didn't just *buy* a Cabbage Patch Kid—they had to *adopt* it. The act of adoption was a powerful emotional cue that created the aura of true parenthood for the child. The doll was as much in need as Roosevelt's bear cub. To prove its parentless status, a Cabbage Patch Kid came with adoption papers and a birth certificate. The doll's arms were outstretched, as though waiting for its new adopted mother to pick it up from the store aisle and take it to a warm, inviting home. The doll was said to have been "born" at Babyland General Hospital. That gave it a real place of origin.

Cabbage Patch Kids circa 1980s. Courtesy of Original Appalachian Artworks
Inc.

The new baby would even get a birthday card after one year. The manufacturer also used technology to mass produce dolls that were one-of-a-kind, just like real babies, with unique names and features. This was important because it greatly heightened the realism of the mom-child relationship. The dolls were also not the prettiest on the market, not by a long shot. They were pudgy and wrinkled, but rather than be thought of as unattractive, these features simply made the dolls appear cuter and more in need. "Love me!" they seemed to shout. "Adopt me!" they seemed to plead.

All of the components coalesced into a simple proposition: a real baby in need motivates a real parent to step up to satisfy those needs. Cabbage Patch Kids *transformed* millions of girls into caring mothers on an unprecedented scale (and transformed many boys into dads, too). Cabbage Patch Kids not only made children happy but many parents also, because the dolls brought children closer to the parenting experience.

I had the pleasure of meeting Xavier Roberts. I presented to him many years ago as part of Ogilvy and Mather's advertising team. Our aim was to bring his business to our client Mattel (and we got it). The thing that struck me most about Mr. Roberts was that Cabbage Patch Kids *were* his children. He treated them as such and not as mere *dolls*. He expected us to treat them that way as well. Beyond the physical features, it was the Cabbage Patch Kids' persona that he crafted. Too often today, toymakers spend enormous resources adding bells and whistles to dolls while paying only secondary attention to the persona that is being shaped. If the toymaker crafts the right nurturing persona, and does it well, it brings out the nurturer in the child, thus helping the child to better satisfy the longing for and excitement of parenthood.

Xavier Roberts said in a statement provided for this book:

Cabbage Patch Kids offered unconditional love and were adopted into families. The millions of children who made that commitment were very good parents. Adoptive parents, to this day, can tell me the name, a detailed description, as well as how they got their very first "baby." With distinctive names, birth dates, and a variety of physical features, Cabbage Patch Kids offered young people a sense of responsibility, individuality, and personalization in what was fast becoming an anonymous, mass-market world.

Cabbage Patch Kids dolls were *on emotional target.* And rather than going with the flow of creating mass-market products, the brand opted for individuality, which heightened the emotional experience. In many ways, it was *antitrend,* because the trend of the day (i.e., mass produced, one size fits all, mechanical products) was interfering with the emotional connection between toy and child.

Xavier Roberts not only created millions of Cabbage Patch Kids, he transformed millions upon millions of children into happy, adoptive parents. That's the point.

Rescuing Puppies

Every one of us has probably walked through a dog pound to select our new pup. It's not always a joyful experience, because they are on death row. Barking, whining, and scratching on fences, dogs at the pound are yearning for someone to take them home. And they may not realize just how vitally important it is to them.

When I was growing up, all of our dogs came from the pound, and each time we took a pup away, I felt great joy that I saved a new friend. I also felt sadness because of all the pups I had to leave behind. To this very day with my own kids, I refuse to buy our dogs at fancy pet stores where pedigrees come with official papers and family histories. I take my kids to the pound, where mongrels are looking for their last hope. Give me the dogs with little chance left. That's how my family found our current dog. In 1994, after our dog, Rooster, passed away, my wife and I took our two children to the pound. There, hundreds of dogs begged for attention. As my family ran from one cage to the next, reaching for the dogs that were beckoning to them, I noticed one dog that did not even try to gain our interest. There was something in that dog's eyes that said all hope was lost. Even as I came close, the pup only held her head up slightly and with caution, afraid that some greater tragedy was soon to befall her. After some coaching, she came over, warily sniffed my hand, and then gave it a brief, tentative lick. She was a mix (a mutt), some cross between a Dalmatian and an English sheepdog. Though Dalmatians of any mix are known to be a bit hyper, this dog had lost all of her enthusiasm. The light was gone from her eyes. She put her head back down even as the other dogs continued to bark and prance about to gain my family's attention.

"Over here!" I shouted. My family immediately fell in love with the hopeless one and named her Lucky. This story is not unusual. Too many dogs need homes, and there are too few homes to accommodate all of them. It's also true that children have an abundance of love to offer and can find it within their hearts to have a multitude of puppies, should such a puppy be in need.

In that larger context, Mike Bowling invented Pound Puppies in 1985. With variations in eyes, ears, colors, and such, he created a brand of plush dogs that needed to be rescued from the pound. They desperately needed a warm home and someone to love and nurture them. Children would visit toy stores, adopt their new pets, and whisk them home. By 1986, Pound Puppies became a worldwide blockbuster toy. They connected with that part of the child that has a reservoir for caring. Pound Puppies transformed children into saviors, nurturers, and dog owners. Pound Puppies were *on emotional target,* using many of the same cues as the Teddy Bear and Cabbage Patch Kids. Pound Puppies simply used a different persona born out of a uniquely different, real-life context (the pound), a context that multitudes could relate to and abhor. Children were suddenly able to feel the thrill of saving puppies. This was especially important in those homes where parents would not allow real dogs, or more of them, anyway. It was uniquely *on trend* in this regard. And as a result, while many plush dogs were available in toy stores, it was Pound Puppies that children decided to save. In so doing, millions of children got to satisfy a part of their nurturing instincts in ways that had not been achieved before, and that brought happiness and smiles to a world of kids.

Nurturing Colonies

Few toys actually provide the ability to nurture a life. In the previous chapter we discussed the Sea Monkeys brand, which would fit this description. Another began in the mid-1950s with Milton Levine. Mr. Levine wondered what it would be like to give children the opportunity to take care of an actual life. This was not just any life, but an industrious one. The idea came to him while he watched ants tunneling their way about his yard in Studio City, California. He decided to bring these amazing creatures to children so that they could own them, see them grow, observe their industrious nature, and nurture them along the way. Milton Levine created Uncle Milton's Ant Farm® brand habitats (Ant Farm is a registered trademark of Uncle Milton Industries, Inc.).

The Uncle Milton's Ant Farm brand habitats concept was—and is—amazingly novel. The child buys the farm (sand encased in plastic with a farm atop) and then sends away for thirty live ants that soon arrive in a tube. The ants enter their new home and begin to dig, tunnel, and create their own city to the amazement of children, who feed them. What made it so special for its day was that for the first time, perhaps, a nurturing toy was created that would appeal to the rough and tumble sensibilities of a boy! Ants were not frilly, snuggly creatures or dolls. They were no-nonsense, nose-to-the-grindstone insects and a tad scary at that. The great benefit was that a boy could connect with his nurturing side without any of his buddies accusing him of being a wimp. It became clear that tough pets

Uncle Milton's Ant Farm® brand habitats. Courtesy of Uncle Milton Industries, Inc. Ant Farm is a registered trademark of Uncle Milton Industries, Inc.

for tough boys could *transform* boys into gentle nurturers. The brand coaxed the nurturer out of the boy in a way that was publicly acceptable for him, placing it right *on emotional target*. It was also a toy that dads could readily appreciate, placing it on their emotional radar as well.

Uncle Milton's Ant Farm brand habitats were also created at a time to take advantage of the political and entertainment landscape. During the fifties and sixties, Hollywood produced a rash of low-budget science-fiction films depicting killer insects. Many times, the creatures in these films were said to have been inadvertently created from the fallout of atomic-bomb tests, a side effect of the arms race with the former Soviet Union. One film in particular became a classic of the genre. Entitled *Them!*, it was about giant ants that took over the sewer system in a community near the Mojave Desert. They wrought havoc and, of course, ate a few people in the process. For a boy, such films made ants appear to be pretty cool creatures to have running around in your bedroom. *Them!* premiered in 1954 and was a success. Uncle Milton's Ant Farm brand habitats were launched in 1956, also to success, placing the toy's genesis squarely *on trend*. Millions have been sold over the years. To this day, about 30,000 Uncle Milton's Ant Farm brand habitats are still sold each month, along with 900,000 ants.

Techno Nurturing

The mold as to what constitutes a nurturing toy was truly cracked in 1996, when inventive minds demonstrated that needy playthings can be created in various guises. That was the year the world was swept away by a tiny, electronic device called Tamagotchi (released in the United States in 1997). Lori Moreno, senior marketing manager of Bandai America Incorporated, says:

> Tamagotchi, Japanese for "lovable egg," was an electronic version of a pet housed in a colorful plastic shell. With a pull of a plastic tab on its side, a virtual pet was hatched—a small creature from outer space displayed on the tiny machine's screen. Like a real pet, the Tamagotchi needed plenty of attention. If it had food, playtime, or discipline needs, it made beeping sounds that persisted if it was ignored. Kids fell in love with Tamagotchi because it filled a void for those who wanted a pet but couldn't own one because of space or financial constraints. It was an instant hit for parents because they loved the fact that kids learned about responsibility without the messy consequences associated with real pets.

Because the Tamagotchi added cues that mimic real babies, it helped children get even closer to the parenting experience, placing it uniquely *on emotional target*. Because it was based on

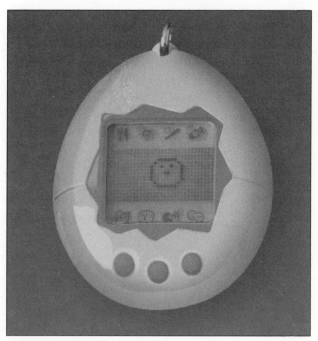

Original Tamagotchi, 1996. Courtesy of Bandai America Incorporated.

burgeoning high-tech gadgetry, it was uniquely *on trend*. The added beauty of Tamagotchi was that it appealed to both genders. Girls liked it because it allowed them to feel like real moms who needed to provide real, constant care. Boys liked it because it was technology driven and provided a touch of game play, giving them the permission to nurture it. And like marbles, it was small enough to be carried about, making it a highly visible and social activity, which spawned word of mouth. It became a worldwide blockbuster toy, one of the top selling of 1997.

A toy brand known as Furby followed soon thereafter in 1998. Invented by David Hampton and marketed by Tiger Electronics, Furby was a furry, gremlin-looking creature, some five inches tall. Stuffed with technology that put it also *on trend,* it would interact with children as well as with other Furbys. Furby would begin by speaking a foreign language (Furbish), though it would eventually begin to speak English. It could also sing, dance, chatter, sneeze, giggle, speak more than eight hundred phrases, blink its eyes, and respond in one way or another to a child's touch. It could quiver with contentment when its stomach was tickled while telling its owner that it loved him. Furbys could also get angry if the child did not play with them enough. All of these realistic temperaments and more made Furby feel very real to children. In turn, it made children feel more like nurturers, albeit to this rather strange creature. Consumer demand skyrocketed, Furby prices rose, and shoppers became frustrated trying to find one at any price. Furby was a blockbuster toy in its first year, selling millions of units.

Nurturing Everywhere

Just as with mastery and creativity, skillful toymakers have learned that nurturing can make for blockbuster toys, but only if the plaything is able to help the child come closer to a realistic nurturing relationship than other toys have been able to achieve. It's important to note that the basic ideas behind the Teddy Bear, Cabbage Patch Kids, Pound Puppies, Uncle Milton's Ant Farm brand habitats, Tamagotchi, and Furby are thousands of years old: create a creature worthy of being loved, add unique product cues that lead to a more realistic parent-child play pattern, use material or technology or entertainment that is *on trend,* and, in so doing, transform the child into a nurturer in ways that were not previously achieved.

The Next Big Thing: Basic Principles

• Invent a toy that more realistically resembles or acts like a creature in need, and you will transform the child into a nurturer and parent. Such a toy allows the child to satisfy the inner need to help, comfort, and nurture. If done in a way that parents find acceptable and appropriate, it might even touch the nurturer within the parent as well.

• Do not start with the product's features but with its persona, and then let the features and play patterns spring from that.

• Do not be overly influenced by the traditional aspects of baby-doll play. Kids can readily accept and identify with nurturing elements in all things, from strange new technologies to ants that burrow under the ground. That leaves the options wide open to create a toy that can bring out the nurturing persona in all children, girls and boys, young and old.

CHAPTER 6

Create an Emulator

All of us strive to emulate others. We find traits we admire in people and we do what we can to attain them. In an adult world, that might include emulating figures related to history, politics, business, religion, and entertainment. Children, too, seek to emulate others. It's a way for children to both learn the world around them and dream about what they might become in that world. While most adults' careers and lifestyles are pretty much fixed, children's are not, and so they use emulation as a way to try on various careers and lifestyles to see what fits. Children can emulate many people and characters in the course of one day as they fantasize about the multitude of life's options. It is all a part of both learning and play. Certainly, the examples we have discussed so far in this book have included elements of emulation, such as the desire to become a master, creator, or nurturer. But this chapter will focus upon those toys that have created actual personas and lifestyles that children have fancifully sought to mimic. The toys that did the best job of helping children imagine what they might be like when they are older (the transformation) have become blockbuster toys. Once again, much of the discussion will revolve around the context in which these toys were introduced that helped place them *on emotional target, on trend,* and so forth.

Blockbuster Women

In the world prior to the 1950s, many thought that little girls should grow up to be mothers and little else. One of the dominant toys of that period was the baby doll, with which girls pretended to be mothers. While that was—and remains—a noble and worthwhile option, it was only one of the many dreams that little girls were beginning to aspire toward. The world was shifting, but baby dolls were not shifting with it. Two world wars demonstrated that when men went off to fight, women were highly successful in keeping industry humming back at home. They were innovative, productive, and immensely capable beyond the mothering duties alone. Women proved that they had a pent-up desire to do more and be more, should they choose. They had options during those times. But when the men came back from fighting World War II, they took the jobs that the women had successfully managed for the years they were absent and sent the women back into the home to be moms, thus creating the baby boom. The daughters of these women, the baby boomers, ached to be and do more if they chose. But the television shows they watched did not reflect this, for women were depicted as stay-at-home moms. Their playthings still did not reflect this, as the toys were still predominantly baby dolls. But these girls' dreams could not be so confined. That was the important context in which the world's most successful blockbuster toy—of all time—was born.

In 1959, Ruth Handler made her vision reality—to give girls an opportunity to live out a multitude of dreams. Ms. Handler invented the Barbie doll. It was the right doll at the right time to ignite pent-up need to achieve. It addressed an emotional need that had been ignored, born out of an emerging social trend. The introduction of the Barbie doll was squarely *on emotional target* and *on trend*. While baby dolls were about caring for another, the Barbie doll was about caring for your aspirations. Through Barbie, little girls found a way to play out their many

1959 Barbie doll. Courtesy of Mattel, Inc.

dreams. While the Barbie doll began life as a teenage fashion model, over time she became involved with a plethora of activities, lifestyles, and professions that little girls could "try on." Girls could pretend to be nurses, doctors, astronauts, business executives, fashion models, rock stars, and, yes, many girls also played "mother" with Barbie (though Barbie was never portrayed as pregnant by the manufacturer). Girls could pretend to surf, go camping, drive boats, own mansions, ride horses, or run ice-cream shops. Certainly, girls had such dreams without Barbie, but the doll helped bring girls closer to the fantasy by laying an amazing array of tangible options at their feet. The

Barbie brand made it easier for girls to connect with their many dreams, and in so doing, Barbie brought out the emulator that was held captive within millions of girls around the world. The fanciful life surrounding the Barbie doll helped transform children from fun-loving little girls into fun-loving women (in their playful fantasies).

Barbie has her critics. Some say she is too pretty and shapely, which creates unattainable expectations (interestingly, Ruth Handler got the idea for the Barbie doll when she saw a sexy German doll named Lilli sold to adults). Some also say that Barbie's world is too lavish, which might feed the growth of materialism. Critics of the Barbie doll fall into the trap of judging her by looks alone or the number of "things" she owns, while conveniently ignoring her positive-role-model elements and the broader context in which she was introduced (a world in which girls' aspirations were often limited solely to motherhood). It's true that many girls consider Barbie to be beautiful and they like all of her "stuff." But if she was enjoyed for her beauty and "stuff" alone, it's doubtful that she would have been as successful as she is. The Barbie doll survived year after year not only because of her looks, but because of her vocations. As girls tried on new aspirations, from being president of the United States to being Olympians, Barbie was there to help them emulate. That's why Barbie has been an amazing success year after year. She reflected the times by changing to meet girls' soaring aspirations, while always staying true to her core reason for being: to help girls fantasize about life's potential. In this regard, the Barbie doll has been the most *regenerative* toy of all time. She is flexible enough to be reinvented each year to reflect major trends and timely fads.

It's helpful to remember that Barbie was not created by an international conglomerate but by a mother and astute businesswoman (Ruth), inspired by her daughter's (Barbara) play with paper dolls of the period. In 1959, the company that Ruth and Elliot Handler founded, Mattel, sold some 351,000 Barbie dolls at $3 each for a total of about $1 million. Barbie annual sales today are approaching $2 billion. It has been deemed the most successful toy of all time. The great majority of parents today buy their daughters a Barbie, and the great majority of girls play with her. Many baby-boomer moms played with Barbie when they were young, too. Over a billion dolls (Barbie, family, and friends) have been sold in about 150 countries. By any definition, this is the blockbuster toy that other blockbusters greatly admire.

A blockbuster toy in the making is the Bratz doll. Introduced in Spain in June 2001 by MGA Entertainment Inc. and later that year in the United States, they became an immediate sensation because of a distinct attitude and fashion sense that appealed strongly to older girls who are age eight to twelve, teen-wannabes. The dolls have edgier features than other fashion dolls, such as pouty lips, platform shoes, hip huggers, and tube tops. It's a clear demonstration that girls have many dimensions to their own personas and attitudes, and they gravitate toward those toys that allow them to safely experiment with those attitudes. By the end of 2002, approximately 12 million Bratz fashion dolls were reportedly sold, and dozens of licensees had signed up to offer girls a multidimensional Bratz experience, ranging from video games to home videos. Just as crafting the right persona was important in the creation of the Cabbage Patch Kids, it is equally important in the creation of emulation figures. It is the persona that the features and play pattern are built to reinforce. To keep the Bratz doll fresh, MGA Entertainment Inc. will need to reinvent it each year to reflect trends and timely fads. It's off to a great start.

Though dolls such as Barbie and Bratz allow girls to more easily touch their many fantasies, it should never be thought that mothering and nurturing are less important in today's world. The previous chapter demonstrated just how important those remain. Another blockbuster toy took form in 1963 at a time when Mom dominated the kitchen (and, in many households today, she still does). That was the year the Easy-Bake

Bratz dolls, 2001. Courtesy of MGA Entertainment Inc.

Oven brand was introduced to the world. As little girls desired to emulate the most important person in their world—Mom— the Easy-Bake Oven allowed them to come closer to the fantasy. In fact, the Easy-Bake Oven allowed little girls to cook *for real*. As we have seen in previous chapters, the closer a brand can bring a child to his or her fantasies, the more likely it is that the brand will become a blockbuster toy. Instead of just emulating Mom in fantasy, little girls got to emulate her in reality. With a sixty-watt bulb serving as the toy's heat source, little girls could cook cakes and be real chefs. They got to mix the batter, pour it into the cake pan, slide it into the oven, watch it bake, take it out, let it cool, and then eat it. The child becomes the creator (see chapter 4) and emulator all at once. The Easy-Bake Oven is truly a blockbuster toy. While the Barbie doll reflected changing attitudes, the Easy-Bake Oven reflected the status quo. Both arenas provide fruitful insights when one is looking to invent the Next Big Thing.

Blockbusters that Triumph

Boys sometimes prefer to achieve different things than do girls, often as a result of thousands of years of acculturation. This has had a vast impact upon the nature of their toys and the icons they sometimes wish to emulate. As we have done before, we need to put such toys, particularly the blockbuster ones, into a broader context.

For thousands of years, boys were expected to grow into men who would protect their families, homes, and empires from those who sought to destroy them. This was a vastly important role in all societies, from the ancient Egyptians to the Chinese, Greeks, Romans, Zulus, Aztecs, and so many more. So it is not surprising that toy soldiers of various types have been found in archaeological digs all around the world. These playthings were not just for fun but a way for parents to begin preparing their sons for adulthood, when they would be *expected and obligated* to protect their homelands for real. Boys did grow into warriors in those days, not just as a full-time profession but even as "occasional" warriors when needed to protect what was theirs. The sad truth is that the world has not changed nearly as much as we would like to imagine. Two world wars happened less than a hundred years ago, a mere moment in the historical record. Regional conflicts happen to this day. Terrorism is now an ever-present reality. And in many countries, boys are still expected to become warriors, if not to confront foreign evils then to confront those that exist in their own neighborhoods.

Even in periods of relative peace, boys will play good vs. evil, pretending to vanquish those who would harm them, their families, and even the world. When conflicts around the world occur, it cannot be hidden from them. They see it on the news at home. They write current-events reports about it in school. They see soldiers in uniforms on the streets. They know of relatives who are now serving. They watch soldiers in national parades. They see them honored on special holidays. With such images, how can we ever expect boys not to imagine that they might go off to battle in order to protect their homeland, to right the world's wrongs, and to destroy the evils that cannot be averted with negotiation? And so, along with so many other options they have before them, boys will pretend to be warriors who vanquish the world's evils. It's pervasive. Many parents, this one included, can feel very uncomfortable with this notion, and I'll raise this "discomfort" again in chapter 18, "Creating Destiny." But for now, realize that boys love to play the hero, and they often do that by thwarting evil.

In the modern era of toymaking, and in the historical and contemporary context discussed, wooden, lead, and tin soldiers were commonplace. They helped boys pretend to be warriors. But the massive explosion in toy soldiers occurred when they were produced in plastic. Known simply as Army Men, they became blockbuster toys during the 1950s and 1960s. They were often only a couple of inches high, came in a wide variety of themes (e.g., WWII, Knights, Civil War, etc.), and were often sold several figures to a bag, which allowed boys to create mock battles. Because of their size, they were highly portable (like marbles), and kids carried them from friend's house to friend's house to play, thus making it a social block-buster as well. The child could recreate a battle and emulate the heroism of brave, valiant men. And that was the point. Playing army is often about playing bravery. It's about the child's ability to vanquish evil and, in the process, feel more powerful in a world in which children can oftentimes feel powerless.

But the small, plastic Army Men that were manufactured in the fifties and sixties were not "poseable." That put limits on a boy's emulative expression. Poseable soldiers would not be introduced until the early sixties. That's when a toy soldier was created as a prop to promote a television show called "The Lieutenant." That idea led Hasbro in 1964 to create its own twelve-inch figure with nearly two dozen movable parts. The movable parts were significant, as they allowed boys to create more realistic poses and thus better imagine the battle and emulate the action. G.I. Joe was born. He was the first true action figure. Unlike the earlier, molded-plastic Army Men, G.I. Joe also had clothes and accessories that boys could play with, thus heightening the realism of the fantasy even further, putting the toy *on emotional target*. Like no other warrior figure before it, G.I. Joe *transformed* boys into pretend warriors. The introductory line had seventy-five different items across four types of fighting men: soldier, marine, sailor, and pilot.

G.I. Joe was also introduced into a specific context. Still fresh from World War II and the Korean War, the United States was embroiled in Vietnam during the time of G.I. Joe's launch. Real U.S. soldiers were in harm's way. These were older brothers, cousins, neighbors, and friends. G.I. Joe was introduced at a time when being a soldier was a very evident profession to emu-late, placing it *on trend* (as unfortunate as that trend might have

G.I. Joe, 1964. From the author's personal collection.

been). As the war wound down, G.I. Joe struggled to remain a bestseller and began to reflect new realities and contemporary themes. He became an adventurer of sorts, going on expeditions in mummy tombs and even battling alien beasts in space. Though sales have risen and fallen over the years, G.I. Joe remains a warrior that boys will still turn to to emulate.

Other characters rose to prominence in the eighties and nineties, when worldwide conflicts were less evident. They were based upon far more fanciful characters. Their very rise to prominence suggests that boys will continue to emulate warriors whether a real-life conflict exists or not. That led the way for He-Man, the central action figure in the Masters of the Universe line. It reenergized the male action category in the early 1980s. From a boy's perspective, He-Man had it all: muscles, weapons, and fortitude to take on the most hideous of evils . . . Skeletor. He-Man and Skeletor battled for supreme control of an entire universe, and nearly every boy enlisted into the noble cause. "I have the power!" was chanted by every would-be hero. The characters had plenty of action features to heighten the play, like power punches (the figures twisted at the hips and sprang about), water sprays, and slime-producing accessories. Though seemingly trivial, the addition of these more action-oriented abilities allowed boys to feel more like heroes than they felt with previous warrior toys, placing the toy highly *on emotional target*. It undoubtedly helped that more fanciful warrior movies were making their way to the theaters at the same time, such as *Conan the Barbarian* in 1982, starring Arnold Schwarzenegger. That placed He-Man *on trend*. The toy line was renewed for several years by introducing new good and evil characters with even more unique, action-oriented powers, thus helping He-Man remain *regenerative*. It even led to the introduction of She-Ra in 1985. As He-Man's sister, She-Ra also battled galactic evil, and little girls could emulate her triumphs. But at its core, He-Man demonstrated that children wanted to emulate powerful characters, even though those characters may be fantasy oriented.

After He-Man began to wane (though there have been a couple of attempts at revival to this very day), other fanciful characters and toys achieved blockbuster status. Introduced in 1984, Transformers are robots that transform from one item (e.g., warrior robot) to another (e.g., warrior vehicle). That added another dimension to emulation. A child could imagine transforming into multiple types of warriors. It also provided a good opportunity for mastery as the child learned how to make the transformation happen.

Teenage Mutant Ninja Turtles were introduced as an entertainment property and became toys in 1988. They had strength, weapons, and bravery. They were turtles, which made them rather unique warriors. But they had something more: a teenage attitude. Like teenagers, they ate pizza, made wisecracks, talked like surfers, loved music, and were cool. This was special because it captured a relevant persona for boys, one that greatly heightened the emotional connection to the characters. Boys could see their future teenage selves in the attitudes these Turtles displayed. It was a double whammy (teens *and* heroes) and a huge success, turning the Turtle Team of Donatello, Leonardo, Raphael, and Michaelangelo into blockbuster toys. They were *on emotional target* in a way no action warriors had been before. Though they, too, waned, they have made attempts at comebacks as well.

In 1993, another entertainment property brought action heroes one step closer to reality: Mighty Morphin Power Rangers. Like other warriors before them, they battled evils to save Earth, though this time the villains were strange-looking space aliens. Like Teenage Mutant Ninja Turtles, these Power Rangers were teens. However, the teens on the television show were portrayed as people (no turtles allowed). With toys in hand, boys could pretend to emulate real teenagers and warriors all at once. These teens also had a social fabric that held the group together, as teens do. Teenage girls were also cast as Power Rangers over the years, which gave girls someone to emulate while connecting to the broader societal trend toward

Original Power Rangers action figure line, 1993. Courtesy of Bandai America Incorporated.

girl empowerment. Power Rangers were uniquely *on emotional target* and *on trend*. They continue to this day because they have been periodically reinvented to provide a sense of newness, making Power Rangers one of the longest-running, *regenerative* male action franchises in existence. Matthew Golding, director of marketing, Bandai America Incorporated, says:

> Kids love Power Rangers because each season brings a new cast of teenagers who band together to save the world from evil space aliens—using their fast vehicles, cool weapons, and powerful megazords. Additionally, the show's timeless themes of teamwork, loyalty, and the victory of good over evil are relevant and make sense to young children. The Power Rangers toy brand continues to be successful because kids strongly identify with these themes and enjoy role-playing the good guys triumphing over the bad guys! Keeping this classic play pattern in mind, Bandai expands the line each year with innovative and realistic toys that allow children to safely explore their superhero fantasies. We refresh the line each season with action figures, innovative megazords, vehicles, role-play weapons, and play sets that bring the television show to life.

Heroes come in all shapes, sizes, fantasies, and realities. Recognizing this, Fisher-Price introduced in 1998 a line of toys based upon a long-overdue hero: Rescue Heroes. These action figures include firefighters, policemen, astronauts, Coast Guard, physicians, and others. They're a wonderful addition to the breadth of heroes already available, made from a simple yet keen insight: true heroes are among us if only we take the time to recognize and appreciate them. This is more evident with the rise of terrorism and the need to protect one's homeland. They provide a nice alternative to parents who feel uncomfortable with the more warriorlike action figures. This helps Rescue Heroes be *on emotional target* and *on trend* with the needs many parents express today.

Many of the previously discussed action figures were supported by entertainment properties of one sort or another. This had a dramatic impact upon their success as toys. More of this will be discussed in later chapters, but their underlying success was related to a boy's need to save the world, a need that has survived and has been cultivated over eons.

Games that help a child emulate such heroes can become blockbusters. One is a naval combat game where each player is in charge of their respective "fleet" of five ships. Each player has a ten-by-ten grid that they can use to guess the location of the enemy fleet. Statements of "hit" and "miss" tell the would-be admiral if they struck their target in this game called Battleship. Various versions of Battleship have been introduced, including one on CD-ROM. Regardless of the version, Battleship allows children to emulate real admirals in a fanciful, safe way. They get to be transformed in fantasy, experiencing the thrill of a victory at sea.

Emulative Fantasies Galore

Children emulate those things they see and, for various reasons, either admire or simply wish to "try on." A great many toys and games have been derived from these simple but enduring fantasies. As mentioned earlier, pretend play is a safe method for a child to experiment with various personas and lifestyles to see what fits, or what might fit, if they had the chance. And once again, the birth of blockbusters is often related to great underlying needs, and sometimes immense historical shifts and context.

In 1934, in the midst of the Great Depression, Charles Darrow was an unemployed engineer. Soup lines were as long as unemployment lines. The downtrodden masses could sometimes catch a glimpse of those who were far better off, and that made them long even more for a chance to be better off, too. During this period of economic collapse, Mr. Darrow developed a game that was, in fact, a version of an earlier board game called "The Landlord's Game," created by Elizabeth Magie in 1904. Charles' game provided a fanciful escape to a better life filled with wealthy real-estate properties, railroads, and energy companies. It allowed the players to gain riches and squash their competition in the process, using the major corporate entities of the period. His game was so complicated and long that, when he brought it to Parker Brothers in 1934, the company identified some fifty-two design problems. So Charles sold his game himself, and when he demonstrated success, Parker Brothers decided to buy it one year later. Charles' game allowed people to own a piece of corporate America, if only in their dreams. The game, of course, was Monopoly. During the greatest depression of our times, it turned out to be the best-selling game. Monopoly touched a place in the hearts of millions who wished they could be millionaires at a time when there was not enough to eat. It was *on emotional target* and *on trend*. Over the years, though the economy has rebounded, Monopoly still fulfills the average Joe's need to emulate the very rich. As adults have such dreams, it is no wonder that many of our children should have the same. Monopoly is the game by which those dreams can, through fantasy, feel real. That's why it's undoubtedly the greatest blockbuster game ever created. It has sold a couple of hundred million copies around the world. Monopoly is not a game that is played. It is a game that *transforms* people into millionaires, if only in their dreams.

In the late 1800s and early 1900s, the mode of long-distance land travel was the iron horse. The person in charge of the iron beast was the engineer, who tended to the train, checked its gauges, and finessed its power and speed as it charged along tracks that united an entire nation. The train took on mythical proportions in those days. It was a mode of romantic and sometimes dangerous adventure, taking its passengers to places never before seen firsthand but only read about in newspapers and dime-store novels of the period. Once again, it was within this grand context that a blockbuster was born. Fascinated with trains since youth, an electrical-products inventor named Joshua Lionel Cowen designed a display as a means to attract passersby into a toy store. The display was an electrical, wooden railroad car that whirled around a road made of metal track and wooden ties. It carried a couple of the store's toys along the circular track, acting as an animated advertisement. The store owner paid Joshua four dollars for the display. The display attracted attention, all right—but not for the store's toys, per se; people wanted to buy the railroad car. What had started out as an advertising ploy turned into a blockbuster toy. "The Electric Express" was born in 1901 and 22,000 electrical cars were sold in the first year. Soon thereafter, everyone wanted their own electric train. With a Lionel train, any child could imagine being an engineer, traveling to faraway places they had never been. In that sense, it was not just a train but a path toward touching one's dreams. Lionel trains *transformed* children into adventurers, in their own basements. Because Lionel took pains to make his trains realistic, it added to the thrill and the fantasy. As other modes of transportation in the real world arrived, the charm and mystery of train travel diminished. But the toys are still enjoyed as much

Lionel train, 1922. Courtesy of Lionel L.L.C.

by dads who owned them decades ago as by their sons who continue to find train travel a marvel. More than 50 million Lionel train sets have been sold since 1901.

As trucks began to pour across America, taking goods from one end of the nation to another, children scrambled to emulate those who drove them. Tonka Trucks was born. They were *on trend*. They were the brainchild of Minnesota teachers in 1947 who, having failed to launch a gardening-tools business, decided to convert the materials into toy trucks. More than 230 million trucks have rolled off the Tonka assembly line since its inception.

But it was cars that children—and society in general— seemed to love most. Growing up, many of us longed for the day when we could own a car. Cars are adult icons of freedom, a rite of passage, and, in some ways, a source and reflection of power, all strong emotional needs. The presence, influence, and romance associated with cars greatly expanded during the 1950s and 1960s as highways grew, production expanded, advertising matured, and consumption flourished. Owning a cool car became one of the earliest status symbols during the past century. It was during this time, when the car was taking on mythic proportions, that two toys were introduced: Matchbox (1954) and Hot Wheels (1968). They were *on trend*. With these toys in hand, children could suddenly better connect with their fantasies of owning and driving automobiles. The toys allowed them to imagine a cool future, in miniature. And so kids asked for and received a multitude of the die-cast wonders. The Hot Wheels track also allowed boys to see just how fast their cars could zoom on straight-aways and loops. Speed was important to the fantasy. The track also brought boys together, as it was the forum through which they could compete to see who had the fastest, coolest cars. Matchbox and Hot Wheels vehicles *transform* kids into car owners and speedsters (if only in fantasy). The toys stayed Ever-Cool (*regenerative*) by introducing new items each year to reflect the fads of the day.

Emulation Everywhere

So many other toys and games allow children to emulate someone. The Operation Skill Game allows children to play doctor, the Magic 8 Ball allows them to play fortuneteller, and Rock'em Sock'em Robots allow them to be prizefighters . . . safely. Allowing children to emulate is powerful, indeed, and can lead to a blockbuster toy, should the focus of the emulation be highly inspirational and should the toy connect with core needs to be *on emotional target* while being *on trend* with society.

The Next Big Thing: Basic Principles

• Invent a toy that more realistically helps children "try on" the lives of their many role models. Help them have fun by safely experimenting with life's many options.

• Find those playful fantasies that children want to fulfill and help them come closer to fulfilling them.

• Keep a watchful eye on massive trends, social movements, and sudden events, so as to quickly ascertain how they may impact children's role models and fantasies.

• As we have discussed before, do not start with the product's features but with its persona, and then let the features and play patterns spring from that in ways that bring the fantasies closer (safely).

• Care needs to be taken when inventing role-model-type toys to ensure that they are, overall, acceptable to parents. The broader the parental acceptance, the more likely it is that the toys will reach blockbuster status. There are some notable exceptions, but such toys tend to have short life spans.

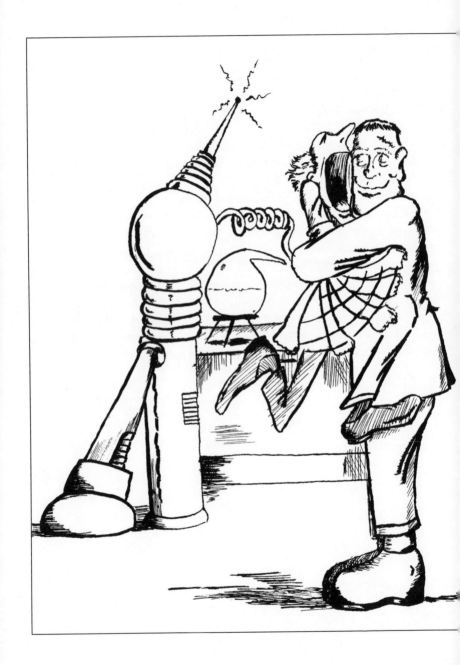

CHAPTER 7

Create a Friend

As we have seen in previous chapters, some toys became blockbusters because they exuded a carefully crafted persona, which was then brought to life with key features and play patterns that served to transform the child. Cabbage Patch Kids perfected the persona of a child in need of adoption and, in so doing, better transformed the child into the fantasy of a parent. G.I. Joe action figures perfected the persona of the noble warrior and, in so doing, better transformed the child into the fantasy of a warrior who would defend his homeland from evil. They were not only *on emotional target* but also *on trend* with the events of the day.

Another persona that some toymakers have crafted is that of good friend, and when this is done well, the child is transformed into the toy's friend. This represents a need as vital as the other personas. We all need friends and a sense of belonging. But for children, friendship is even more vital because the world is big and they are small. Friendship provides someone they can talk to, relate to, share with, learn from, and laugh with. Friends provide someone the child can confide in. Children can express their fears to friends, tell their secrets to them, and say things that they would not dare tell others. Toys that have been a child's friend, and have done so better than other toys, have become blockbuster toys.

The Raggedy Truth

Born in 1880 in Illinois, Johnny Gruelle was a political cartoonist and illustrator of children's stories. One day, his daughter, Marcella, found a rag doll in the attic and brought it to him. It was in pretty poor shape and had no face. The family added black shoe buttons for eyes and a triangle nose. Johnny Gruelle gave the doll a name, Raggedy Ann, which was a combination of two poems of the day, "The Raggedy Man" and "Little Orphan Annie." Gruelle wrote several stories about this character and his daughter, so legend says, to cheer her up because she was ill following an inoculation with the smallpox vaccine. The first book opens with Marcella finding Raggedy Ann in her grandma's attic and bringing it to her. Grandma "hugged the doll to her breast," says the story. She was pleased to be reacquainted with the friend she had as a child. "Raggedy Ann," Grandma said, "you have a new playmate and mistress now, and I hope you both will have as much happiness together as you and I used to have!" With that statement, Grandma handed down her Raggedy Ann to her granddaughter, thus continuing the line of friendship. "Oh, Grandma! Thank you ever and ever so much!" said Marcella. "Raggedy Ann and I will have just loads of fun."

With that introduction, the stories of Raggedy Ann began and continue to this day, living for nearly one hundred years thus far. The books spoke of friendship and of doing the right things in life. Dolls stemming from the Raggedy Ann stories were first created in 1935 by the P. F. Volland toy company. Given the sweet introduction from the books and their persona, they became enduring blockbuster toys. These were not baby dolls that girls might nurture, or fashion dolls that girls might emulate. They were friend dolls, giving children a kind and sweet character they could talk to as a peer, hold as a friend, and confide in. They were *on emotional target*. The world may be scary and the night dark, but they are far less so when a child is holding Raggedy Ann and Andy. They are pals that see a child through the toughest of times and that are there to brighten the best of times. I also think that the doll's "raggedy" nature contributed to its appeal. She has flaws here and there, as all children have, making her very relatable. Moreover, children can bring Raggedy Ann everywhere, for that's what you do with close friends. It should be noted that the real Marcella, still a child of thirteen, died in 1915 of the infection she developed from that smallpox vaccine. But she lives on in stories that bear her name, alongside her best friend, Raggedy Ann.

Bear Friends

Friends can come in all shapes, sizes, and character types. One inventor began with the concept of a bear and then crafted a friendly persona, made unique with technology. It was 1985 when Worlds of Wonder introduced a truly innovative toy in its day, Teddy Ruxpin. Teddy Ruxpin could speak, tell stories, and sing to children, moving his mouth as he did so and opening and closing his eyes. It was an amazingly alive buddy, which was not all that surprising when you realize that a Disney engineer invented the toy. Children would insert a cassette tape into Teddy Ruxpin and the lifelike animated show began. The tapes, and storybooks that came with them, brought kids on adventures, but they often had a moral about friendship. The friendship theme was *on emotional target,* but it was the *on-trend* technology that brought the friend to life. Within one year, Worlds of Wonder had earned several million dollars in profit on approximately 90 million dollars in gross sales. It was the toy of the year and resulted in an animated cartoon show as well. It was also a very expensive toy by the standards in those days. It proved that if you crafted the right persona, and created a point of difference via technology that enhanced the friendship, parents were willing to pay for a quality toy and friend. But sustaining that turned out to be difficult. Worlds of

Wonder went out of business within a couple of years because they could not find a way for the toy to remain contemporary (*regenerative*).

A blockbuster in the making is Build-A-Bear Workshop, a new retail store that allows children "from 3-103 to create their own huggable companions." Children walk into the Build-A-Bear Workshop and literally create a new friend from start to finish, selecting many elements including the bear's body, clothes, and name. The child then stuffs its animal, thus bringing it to life. The process heightens the child's emotional connection to the toy because the child is very involved in creating the new friend. In this way, Build-A-Bear Workshop helps fulfill several emotional needs, including creativity, control, and, of course, friendship. This places it highly *on emotional target*. It demonstrates the power of satisfying various emotional drivers. The company opened its first store in the St. Louis Galleria in 1997 and by the end of 2002 had over a hundred stores. The company's slogan is "Where Best Friends Are Made." How true.

It's interesting to compare the birth of the Teddy Bear with those of Teddy Ruxpin and Build-A-Bear Workshop. All are bears, you might say. But the key points of difference are persona and emotional drivers. The Teddy Bear was born out of the need to be saved, thus requiring it to be nurtured. Teddy Ruxpin and Build-A-Bear Workshop were born with a very different persona: friendship. The first used technology to bring that friendship persona to life in ways not accomplished before, whereas the second used technology to empower children to create their own friend. Technology can "plus" common things to make children's fantasies feel more real. Comparing these three toys also demonstrates that icons such as bears (or space aliens, insects, dinosaurs, etc.) are simply canvases upon which the master toymaker uses persona and technology to put them *on emotional target* and *on trend* in ways that uniquely heighten the emotional connection.

Stuffed bear from Build-A-Bear Workshop. From the author's personal collection.

Fragranced Friends

American Greetings was successful in creating sweet characters that children looked upon as friends. It used those characters primarily for greeting cards and stationery. The most notable was that of Strawberry Shortcake. She was kind, sweet, innocent, and giving. The power of this personable character made it clear that it was destined to become more than a greeting card. American Greetings licensed the character to Kenner to make into a doll, and not just any doll but one that smelled of strawberries, which came right out of its essence. Adding a fragrance was unique for the day, which wasn't so much *on trend* as much as it *created trend*. Strawberry Shortcake also came with plenty of her own friends, like Blueberry Muffin and Lemon Meringue, each scented. The friendly persona of the characters and the fragranced dolls were enough to catapult Strawberry Shortcake to blockbuster status as a blockbuster friend. They sold some 25 million dolls and about $1.2 billion in merchandise, according to one source. The success of the Strawberry Shortcake doll continues to this day. "One of the world's most popular icons from the eighties, little girls loved sharing in the adventures of Strawberry Shortcake and her friends," says Holli Hoffmann, marketing manager, Bandai America Incorporated (the current manufacturer). "While Bandai America's new crop of scented dolls, playsets, and vehicles introduces Strawberry Shortcake with her 'berry' fresh look to a new generation of girls, today's Strawberry Shortcake still retains the innocent, wholesome qualities that originally captured our hearts. She will continue to embody the themes of friendship, adventure, and fantasy play that have timeless appeal for young girls."

Friends that Teach

Children learn things from friends. Friends can teach them how to be friends, how to get along with others, how to have fun, and how to learn and grow. Friends can help children

Strawberry Shortcake, 2003. Courtesy of Bandai America Incorporated.

master the world around them. This is closely related to the ideas brought forth in chapter 3, about how toys can help a child gain mastery over the world. And in turn, they can transform children into friends.

November 1969 is an important date in the history of education born of friendship. That was the moment when a new group of friends blasted onto the children's pop-culture scene. These friends had unlikely names like Bert, Ernie, Cookie Monster, Oscar the Grouch, and, of course, Big Bird. This was "Sesame Street," an urban setting where Muppets mixed with real-life people and where learning became fun, thanks to the brilliance of Jim Henson and the Children's Television Workshop. Songs and comic routines provided a solid foundation for learning that included lessons about ABCs, safety, and even coping with death. The program took an in-depth approach to helping children, served up in a contemporary way, and, in so doing, was *on trend* with childhood needs. The characters were children's trusted friends, and they became a worldwide phenomenon. The executives who guided "Sesame Street" understood that by going through a child's heart, by creating a close friendship connection with these characters, they could better connect with children's evolving intellects to help them learn. It worked on an unprecedented scale. "Sesame Street" has helped to educate more than 100 million children around the world in some 130 nations. It has won over fifty Emmy Awards.

Friends that begin as educational and entertainment properties (in this case, to entertain in order to educate) have the ability to translate into toys. Children want to touch them, squeeze them, and take them places. "Sesame Street," as a brand of toys to help inspire education, is a blockbuster. The toys, in turn, help keep children connected to their friends in ways that foster further education. One of the amazing blockbuster toys under the "Sesame Street" umbrella in recent years is Tickle Me Elmo. In 1996, it was the fifth most popular toy in dollar sales in the United States, selling over 1 million dolls. It rose to be the second most successful toy in 1997, beaten only by Tamagotchi. Children will return friendship with friendship. Tickle Me Elmo also had blockbuster marketing, as well as a large dose of *X Factor,* the unpredictable elements that can sometimes work in a toy's favor. This will be discussed further in a later chapter.

Another child's friend originated from an unlikely source. When you think of dinosaurs, you tend to imagine a T-Rex taller than a house that is fully capable of swallowing any of us whole. But that is not how this dinosaur began. In 1987, a former teacher named Sheryl Leach had quite a different dream. She, along with another teacher named Kathy Parker and producer Dennis DesShazer, invented a dinosaur that would be a child's friend, one that would entertain and educate. They created the purple dinosaur named Barney, launching him into the world of home videos in 1988. "Barney & Friends" was picked up by the Public Broadcasting Service (PBS) in April 1992. Barney is a friend to children everywhere. He teaches them how to sing, have fun, share, cooperate, have good manners, respect others, take care of their health, and more. That is, after all, what friends do. In return, children were transformed into Barney's friends, so much so that when Barney made the leap from videos to toys, the playthings became worldwide blockbusters, with millions of plush and preschool learning toys sold. After all, children want to hug their friend and keep him close. The plush Talking Barney, in particular, benefited from technology that allowed it to speak hundreds of phrases, not merely a half-dozen, which was common at the time. This heightened the emotional connection and the fantasy by making Barney more real.

Friends across Time

New blockbusters are often formed by mixing and matching common concepts, so as to invent unique combinations that can be added to a child's toy box (more on this in chapter 17). One such brand was born in 1986. This brand took a historical perspective of what it was like to be a girl growing up in various eras in American history. Real girls were allowed to peek into the lives of these peerlike, historical characters and friends through storybooks and exposure to dolls. Girls were able to learn about both the historical contexts and the elements of girlhood and friendship than transcend the years. The American Girls Collection was born of the insightful wisdom of Pleasant T. Rowland. "Our company," says the Pleasant Company, "was founded on the idea that learning about history doesn't have to be boring . . . engaging stories about girls living at important times in the past—and dolls standing as tangible symbols of these characters—could breathe life into history, turning it into something real and personal, something today's girls could hold in their hands."

Through American Girls, girls can learn more about what it is like to be a girl, of any period. Beyond the stories and dolls themselves, American Girls helps today's girls meet life's challenges through insights provided by their Web site and magazine. It is a total concept of friendship. A recent issue of *American Girls* magazine offered girls tips for selecting gifts, cooking, growing up, and throwing a party. In that vein, American Girls is a friend by helping girls with their everyday lives. Mattel, the current owner of the Pleasant Company, states that American Girls is a $300-million division. But more

The American Girls Collection®. Courtesy of Pleasant Company, 8400 Fairway Place, Middleton, WI 53562.

than that, it is a friend that helps girls embrace life. The lesson is this: being a friend doesn't mean making a quick sale. It means understanding children's larger world and the needs that they have, and then seeking ways in multiple mediums—beyond toys—to come to the aid of children. The Pleasant Company succeeded in providing a friend to girls in ways ignored by all other *toy* companies before.

The Greatest Friend of All

The granddaddy of all contemporary kid friends, however, was created by a brilliant and creative man born in a Chicago suburb on December 5, 1901. His early life was spent on the family farm, until 1910, when times turned tough and the family sold it and moved to Kansas City. As the young man grew up, he worked various jobs, such as delivering newspapers and working in a jelly factory. But his dreams were elsewhere. The young man loved to draw, and so he began to pursue that. He enrolled at Chicago's Academy of Fine Arts, but he soon took a break in his studies to join the Red Cross so that he could aid the World War I effort overseas. When he came home, he announced to his father that he was going to become an artist. The announcement didn't go over well, for his father objected to such a frivolous profession. But the young man had made up his mind, so he set out to follow his dream. He initially tried to become a political cartoonist, then settled for a job at an advertising agency, but eventually he began to create movie-theater cartoons. It was the perfect vehicle for his humor and imagination, and the match proved ideal.

A young Walt Disney had found his love. The first series of cartoons were called "Alice Comedies," which used a live actress interacting with cartoon figures. That led to another cartoon character named "Oswald the Lucky Rabbit." But none of these would compare to Walt Disney's greatest creation, a small friendly mouse with human attributes. He was first named Mortimer Mouse, but Walt's wife didn't quite like

Mr. Walt Disney, surrounded by licensed Mickey Mouse plush toys, circa 1930s. Courtesy of The Walt Disney Company. © Disney Enterprises, Inc.

it, so they came up with a far better alternative . . . Mickey Mouse. Two cartoons featuring Mickey Mouse were created, but the one that made the world take notice was called *Steamboat Willie.* That's because it offered a novelty that was *on trend* . . . sound! Mickey Mouse was the first character to be featured in a synchronized-sound cartoon. The impact of this innovation cannot be overemphasized. It helped make the character appear more real, the fantasy more real, and so too his friendship.

Imagine that you are an avid theatergoer on November 18, 1928. You decide that day to see a movie at the Colony Theater in New York City. Most of the movies you see are still silent, though some have added sound. Cartoons were largely silent. Suddenly, as you sit there in the dark, munching on popcorn, Mickey Mouse appears on the large screen and, for the first time ever, you see a cartoon character move to the beat of actual music. You glance at your friends sitting next to you, then back at the screen, then at your friends again . . . amazed. The crowd in the packed theater suddenly lets out a thunderous laugh. It dies down. Then another laugh roars as this mouse's personality, greatly heightened by the addition of sound, pours over the seats, enveloping every single man, woman, and child and creating an everlasting, cemented bond. *Steamboat Willie* was the true birth of Mickey Mouse . . . the friend. So many blockbuster ideas have been born over the years, but the moment of magic is forgotten. That moment for Mickey Mouse was on that fateful day in 1928. A reporter for the *Exhibitor's Herald* wrote, "It is impossible to describe this riot of mirth, but it knocked me out of my seat." *Steamboat Willie* was "an ingenious piece of work with a good deal of fun," the *New York Times* reported. "It growls, whines, squeaks and makes various other sounds that add to its mirthful quality." With a voice, Mickey Mouse had a soul.

Over time, Walt created an array of other heartfelt characters that were connected in friendship. These became classics.

Along with Mickey Mouse, there were Minnie, Daisy, Donald, Goofy, and Pluto. Through stories of their relationships and exploits, kids everywhere came to know these friends and adopted them as friends, too. There is no better expression of this than at a Disney theme park. As costumed characters of Mickey and friends walk through the parks, they are mobbed by children seeking to shake their hands and get hugs. Mickey Mouse has all the virtues that we wish friends to have: kindness, sincerity, loyalty, humor, and comfort.

Mickey Mouse is a worldwide blockbuster character at a level never before achieved and never after paralleled, known by countless children in virtually every country on the face of the earth. It's not surprising, then, that children want to take their friend home and keep him close. The toys that have sprung from Mickey and friends have been blockbusters for decades and have ranged from plush figures to preschool learning toys. But Mickey Mouse is not just a child's friend; he's a friend to all those parents who were once children, too. Parents are often the first to introduce their children to their friend Mickey Mouse, as a way of handing that friendship from one generation to the next. Mickey Mouse, as friend and companion, is simply, amazingly, unprecedented and unmatched.

Says Pam Greer, director of market research at Disney Consumer Products:

> In fall 2002 we had the opportunity to talk to moms, kids, teens, and young adults across the country about their relationship to Mickey Mouse. What we heard was an incredible passion and love of a character that transcends age, gender, and even country of birth. This character, more than any other character, has been invited into people's homes and lives. He is the character moms trust to set a good example, the character that kids trust to be a good friend, and the character everyone counts on to always be there when we need him. Over and over again we heard teens and young adults declare that Mickey should never change, and that he had better be around when they have kids.

One tattooed and pierced teen boy in Berkeley told us, "Mickey is in storage. But he's coming out when I have kids." Mickey has a very special and powerful transgenerational quality.

Ms. Greer kindly provided another quote from a twenty-three-year-old man who doesn't have children: "Mickey is a way to connect with older and younger generations at the same time. My parents know about Mickey, my grandparents know about Mickey, and, of course, I'm going to pass down my experiences to my children."

"For generations," continues Ms. Greer, "people have invited Mickey to be part of their lives. Families use Mickey to help them mark moments of joy in their lives and to help them deal with difficult times. Mickey Mouse has become a part of our personal history in a way no other character can." Here are some more testimonials.

"My seven-year-old has cancer and last Christmas he was in the hospital. I brought him a big Mickey stuffed animal and he sticks with it. At that time, that was something he could cuddle up with and it was important to him" (mom of six- and seven-year-old boys).

"When I was nine or ten years old, my uncle took me and my brothers to Disney World [Walt Disney World Resort] after my dad died to try to make us feel better" (mom of eighteen- and thirty-five-month-olds).

"My twins were in the hospital for eighteen days when they were born and when we got to finally take them home, my girlfriend gave them little caps—a Minnie Mouse cap for my daughter and a Mickey Mouse cap for my son. That was the very first not-hospital clothing that these children had" (mom of children ages three to five).

"I went to boarding school and my mom left a Mickey on my bed. I still have that Mickey Mouse. He's very special to me" (mom of six- and seven-year-old boys).

"In the back room," Ms. Greer concludes, "we found ourselves

moved by the connection that our consumers felt toward
Mickey Mouse. Each story we heard was one of love, respect,
and attachment to the character."

The Next Big Thing: Basic Principles

• Invent a toy that is a friend, but heighten the friendship in
ways not yet achieved by using technology or themes (e.g.,
space, aliens, animals, etc.) that place it *on trend*, while helping
the friendship fantasy appear more real and unique than previously attained. As always, do not start with the product's features but with its persona, and then let the features and play
patterns spring from that.

• Being a child's friend is not merely about creating a toy;
it's about lending aid as a friend would. Find ways to be a
child's friend that transcend the toy. Think about what it
means to be a child's friend in today's world and how your
brand can come to the child's or parent's aid. Good friends
make a child laugh, play, feel comfort, and learn. They make
parents happy and help them in their quest to aid their child
in many ways.

CHAPTER 8

Create a Collector

Children love to collect. It satisfies various needs, for order, pride, expertise, and especially accomplishment. Children have collected coins, insects, baseball cards, and, as it applies to toys, marbles, dolls, plush toys, action figures, and more. This chapter addresses a toy's ability to produce such joy and in a very specific way so that the child will want to own various versions of the same toy. The toy, in effect, moves from mere plaything to blockbuster because it has certain elements that transform children into collectors.

To be a collectible in a child's eyes, a toy must first be worthy of collecting. To begin, like any other blockbuster toy, it must satisfy a deep emotional need within the child. The Barbie doll, as we have seen, helps satisfy a girl's need to aspire; Mickey Mouse, as a plush toy, helps satisfy a child's need for friendship; and Cabbage Patch Kids help satisfy a child's need to nurture. Though some toys may equally satisfy a child's emotional needs, the collectible toy goes further. It has an uncanny way of inspiring the child (and oftentimes the parent) to seek out new varieties each year, to tell their friends about them, to trade them, to read more about them, to share insights about them, and to become an expert on the subject of the toys. Such toys inspire children to become truly passionate about their collection—to become enthusiasts. Different toys have inspired children to become enthusiasts through different means. While the toy must first satisfy an emotional need, as described earlier, it is the avenue the toys take beyond that which sheds light upon how they were able to reach collectible status.

This chapter is about a youth's desire to own multiple toys of the same brand because, together, they often provide a play value beyond their individual worth (one plus one equals three). Not surprisingly, several of the brands already discussed in this book are referenced yet again. It is often the case that great toys employ multiple blockbuster ideas that help them become and stay blockbuster toys as outlined in chapter 2. I decided to break out the collectible nature of these playthings because of the importance it plays in the creation of blockbuster toys.

Creating and Recreating Worlds Creates Collectors

Some toys become collectibles because they reinvent themselves in unique ways every year. The "new" item is made different enough from last year's item within the line. Those toys that change to reflect the times (*regenerative*) have an advantage. Whereas adults often find comfort in the same old thing, and it takes effort to get them to try something new, kids are just the opposite; they embrace newness and shy away from the same old thing. Children want this year's toys and this year's innovations, for those are the items that are talked about on the playground. If the toy is not reinvented to reflect trends and fads, children will deem it as old, and they will not request the following year's new version of that toy, which is the first step toward the formation of the collection. In addition, many toys become collectible because the newer items expand the play pattern significantly. One way to achieve both of these criteria is to uniquely expand the toy's "world." This provides not only a reason for the child to request new toys within the brand year after year but also to request multiple toys of the brand in any given year.

Once again, a great example of a collectible brand is the Barbie doll. The doll satisfies the girl's need for aspiration, but the manufacturer reinvents Barbie each year to reflect contemporary themes. This involves broad social changes (Barbie transforming from nurse to doctor, from stewardess to pilot), fanciful themes (Barbie of Swan Lake), and pop-culture fads (SpongeBob SquarePants Barbie doll). Such changes are significant enough that children will readily "recognize" a difference between what they bought last year and what's offered this year. Barbie offers more than a clothes change; she offers a dream change. Role playing as a doctor acts out a far different dream than role playing as a schoolteacher. In that context, girls are not just collecting Barbie dolls with different outfits; they are collecting different dreams. That's one reason why girls will collect Barbie dolls year after year. The dreams just keep piling up. Such dreams can also be readily displayed on shelves and dresser tops.

The dreams Barbie inspires are not ignited by the Barbie doll alone, but are also brought to life in a world filled with other characters that interrelate with her. This world is important. Ken became her boyfriend in 1961. Midge became her best friend in 1963. Skipper became her little sister in 1964. Kelly became her baby sister in 1995. Children, then, desire to collect multiple characters in order to attain added play patterns that heighten and expand the fantasy scenarios. But the "collectible math" is not simply one plus one equals two. One Barbie doll by itself has a certain play scenario. One Midge doll by itself has a certain play scenario. But Barbie and Midge combined have far more than just two play scenarios. Together, they allow girls to "play out" many social patterns and interrelationships that relate to best-friend issues: sharing secrets, gossiping, talking about boys, trying on each other's clothes, going to a party together, and many more. In this way, one plus one equals at least three and, many times, dozens of new play patterns and ways to have fun. If the child also adds boyfriend

Ken and Barbie's sister dolls, you can just imagine how the play scenarios rapidly expand. That's yet another reason why the Barbie doll can inspire girls to become collectors. The adult might see only three dolls, but the child experiences a multitude of fantasies and play patterns that are *on emotional target.*

But the Barbie brand does more than that. Dreams and interrelationships are heightened when accessories are added to complete the world. For the Barbie brand, these have included boats, automobiles, airplanes, horses, townhomes, ice-cream shops, and much more. Girls collect such Barbie items to complete the fantasy world. It's not about the "toy stuff." It's about the "stuff of dreams." So the child's collection, including interrelating characters and accessories, becomes a world with virtually limitless fantasies and limitless ways to satisfy emotional needs in a fun, fanciful, safe way.

Other brands have been able to turn children into collectors because they too have created a world filled with varied dreams, characters, interrelationships, and accessories. Classic worlds of male action characters such as G.I. Joe and Power Rangers, for instance, provide opportunities for the child to collect the items within the world to enhance the play: good guys, bad guys, vehicles, equipment, and so forth. The greater and more intricate the world, the greater and more intricate the play patterns and the fun. In a marketplace where toys compete for time with a growing array of activity options (from outdoor sports to video games), these expanded worlds help the child stay interested in the brand a little longer. The better the brand has clearly defined characters that connect to different fantasies and provided accessories that help enhance play patterns, the more likely it is that the child will desire to complete the world so as to play within it.

One of the earliest collection crazes in the modern era was toy trains. Children still desire to create the world that includes such items as trains, different engines and railcars, train stations, mountain tunnels, forests, neighborhoods, main streets, miniature people, and even miniature cows that graze near the tracks. The more detailed the world, the more real the fantasy. As mentioned earlier, the Lionel Company took special care to help ensure that their trains approached realism. This allowed the child—and the child in all of us—to touch the realism of the train experience right from our own homes. Satisfying that desire for realism is another way to transform children into collectors. The realism and detail not only heightens the fantasy; it often leads to greater pride and accomplishment, especially when the child collector gets to show off the collection to others.

Competition Creates Collectors

Marbles were probably among the world's first collectible items. Coming in different sizes and colors, they represented an amusing assortment of precious, colorful items to collect and show. One of the elements that helped spur their development into a collection, perhaps, was that they were used as a form of competition. As mentioned in an earlier chapter, if a child plays "for keeps," then the collection is not just a group of pretty marbles but instead a representation of one's winnings, expertise, and accomplishments—the spoils of victory. In that context, marbles take on the exalted status of hard-won trophies. Because they are also highly portable, marbles allowed children to carry them around their townships, show off their winnings, and engage in new competitions in hopes of gaining even greater spoils.

In the modern era, the blockbuster toy that contained the potential for this type of play is Nintendo's Game Boy video-game system, a portable handheld electronic game introduced in 1989. One of the most interesting innovations of the Game Boy system is that two of the devices can be connected with a cord, which allows them to swap information (compete). The Pokemon game, introduced for the Game Boy in 1998, took advantage of this unique feature. Within the game of Pokemon—which stands for "Pocket Monster"—each player is a "trainer" whose goal is to capture and tame monsters (there are about 250 of them) so that he can become the world's best trainer. This connected with many emotional drivers such as mastery, power, nurturing, and victory, all of which helped Pokemon be *on emotional target*. But the collectible nature of the Pokemon monsters added further to the uniqueness and appeal of the game. Each monster had a unique look and power that made it desirable and worth collecting. Each monster would also evolve, which enticed the child to collect them all to see what each became. And no Game Boy Pokemon pack had all of the monsters. To get them all, you had to connect with other players and trade them. To add to the fun and inspire connections, there was one monster called Mew that could be captured when two Game Boy systems were connected, setting the stage for a competition and swapping. These elements pulled players together, which heightened the social fun of the game and inspired passionate collecting. Over the years, over 100 million Game Boy systems have been shipped and over 700 different titles have been introduced in a wide range of genres.

The game of Pokemon, and the technology that the Game Boy system brought to it, in many ways is as ancient as marbles. The differences, of course, are that the game is now electronic and the marbles are themed (monsters), which places them *on trend* for the period; the players know how many they need to collect (the goal); and the game is about an adventure (with capturing, training, and battle elements) and based upon a fantasy in which children can imagine they are transformed into powerful trainers, which places it *on multiple emotional targets*. The success of the toy led to tournaments designed to "crown" the greatest Pokemon Master (the sign of mastery as described in chapter 3) and related merchandise such as collectible trading cards, plush toys, and even a television series and movies. Newer versions of the game were introduced to help it remain contemporary and *regenerative*. The Pokemon phenomenon led to billions in sales and as many smiles, making the Pokemon game itself a true blockbuster. It's a good example of what can occur when a toy franchise fulfills many of the core principles cited in chapter 2.

Retirement Creates Collectors

In 1993, a small but soon to be blockbuster toy was born. It connected with a different set of emotional drivers and used a very different approach to motivate children—and many adults—to become collectors. That was the year that Ty Warner created a modest line of nine baby animal bean bags with the names of Pinchers the Lobster, Flash the Dolphin, Legs the Frog, Squealer the Pig, Brownie the Bear, Splash the Whale, Patti the Platypus, Chocolate the Moose, and Spot the Dog. They were babies, which connected with the nurturing instinct (*on emotional target*). They were cute, which added to the appeal. They were underfilled with plastic pellets, which made them highly squeezable and lovable. They were also highly displayable. They had a low price point (usually five to seven dollars), which made multiple purchases rather affordable. They were Beanie Babies.

While the cute, baby-oriented, displayable, and affordable benefits helped ignite interest in Beanie Babies, there was one added element that led to a rush of intense collecting beyond anything else the toy industry had seen before. Ty decided to "retire" older Beanie Babies, making them scarce and a true collector's item. He managed supply so that demand would always be higher. That pulled not only kids but adult collectors into the market. The hunt was on to grab all of the Beanie Babies off the shelf before they, too, were retired. There was a certain degree of thrill in the hunt. "Look which ones I got" became a source of pride. Retirement of Beanie Babies led to skyrocketing prices as collectors began to bid up the price of rare Beanie Baby items. At the height of the frenzy, one retired Beanie Baby was sold for $13,000. In the fall of 1999 when sales

Beanie Babies. From the author's personal collection.

of Beanie Babies began to slow, Ty announced that on December 31 of that year, all Beanie Babies would be retired. The publicity led to another holiday season of frenzied shopping and collecting, in hopes of obtaining items that might someday be worth a small fortune. In fact, the marketing success of Beanie Babies depended far more upon "the buzz" than upon advertising, a point I will revisit in a later chapter. Though more Beanie Babies were eventually introduced, the intense fervor over Beanie Babies subsided (as with all things), but not before Beanie Babies surpassed $1 billion in sales.

The Next Big Thing: Basic Principles

• First and foremost, invent a toy that is *emotionally on target* and *on trend*, and only then consider if the toy lends itself to being a collectible.

• Consider the many paths that might possibly lead to the desire to collect. These include reinventing the toys each year with discernable differences reflective of trends and fads (*regenerative*), creating worlds of characters and accessories to greatly expand the play scenarios with each added item (one plus one equals many), inspiring fun and friendly competition and swapping, creating toys that are highly portable and displayable, keeping price points low, or retiring items so as to increase their value while ensuring that the market does not become flooded with (tired of) the toy brand (more on this in later chapters).

CHAPTER 9

Create a Story Lover

Stories are as ancient as mankind. The first stories were crafted ages ago, long before the written word was even conceived. Some of these stories were faithfully passed from one generation to the next, making their way into contemporary themes and literature. Stories are rich in meaning. They are used to convey mankind's speculation as to the origin of the universe, to explain the awesome powers witnessed in Nature, to record the history of various peoples, and to convey an evolving sense of morality, right and wrong.

Children are often the audience for such stories, for they are the ones who have the most to learn. Stories are often told in an entertaining way to keep the child's attention and facilitate remembrance. Storytellers held an important position in mankind's early history because they were responsible for shaping the knowledge and beliefs of the youth. They were thought to be imbued with great knowledge, wisdom, and sometimes even supernatural powers.

Native American lore is a prime example of man's immense ability to convey ideas, history, and entertainment through such tales as "The Yellowstone Valley and the Great Flood" (Cheyenne), "The First Fire" (Cherokee), and "A Little Brave and the Medicine Woman" (Sioux). You can just imagine dozens of Native American children sitting around a warm, crackling fire on a cool evening as a storyteller weaves a tale handed down for centuries. Little by little, the attentive children are pulled into the storyteller's embrace, listening to tales that enlighten their minds and spirits. For centuries, this was the storytelling experience all around the world. And those stories that are exceptionally well crafted transform children into attentive story lovers.

For most of the history of toys, however, most playthings did not have stories associated with them. Stories were thought to be quite distinct from toys. Though some ancient toys had play patterns that were storylike, such as ancient toy figures of Roman warriors used to create mock battles, these were less about a story and more a one-note activity. As we look at the blockbuster toys that arose forty or more years ago, such as Erector Sets, Easy-Bake Oven, and Crayola Crayons, we see that all are void of overt story elements. Storymakers and toymakers lived in separate worlds.

Some wonderful characters, such as Mickey Mouse, eventually developed into toys because children fell in love with them. Disney characters were, in fact, some of the first properties that were licensed to become toys. But by and large, developing a story was not really a consideration when developing a toy and vice versa.

The Blockbuster Story that Gave Birth to the Blockbuster Toy

All that changed in May of 1977 when Fox released *Star Wars*. This blockbuster movie demonstrated to both moviemakers and toymakers that if a story satisfies emotional needs in the audience, it can greatly increase the odds that a toy line based upon it will be a blockbuster, too. It showed that a good story can help give birth to a toy line by defining the characters, giving them personas, articulating the role each character plays, providing the vehicles and equipment the characters need, and focusing the goal of the play pattern (in the case of *Star Wars*, good vanquishing evil). In short, the story gives the toy prominence, a reason for being, and a play pattern that helps children emulate a character they admire or a situation they want to confront (emulation as explained in chapter 6).

There are those who will object to this on the grounds that toys based upon movies, storybooks, comic books, and so forth are too commercial, and I will address that point in a later chapter. But for now, realize this: children love stories when they present courageous and noble characters that children can identify with. They love toys when those toys help them "play out" wonderful stories. In that context, the story and the toy can merge in a seamless way to satisfy deeply rooted emotional needs, which are manifested in excitement at the theater and during playtime at home. That's what *Star Wars* did in a big way; it merged the mediums of storytelling and toymaking in a way and on a scale never before achieved. George Lucas created a story with engaging characters that children wanted to emulate in a more intimate way than could be achieved at the theater.

The studio didn't realize the potential of *Star Wars*. In fact, the merchandizing rights for science-fiction films were considered so worthless by the studio (or any studio of that day) that George Lucas easily retained all rights to the merchandise associated with the film. Those rights turned into billions of dollars. Toys based upon Luke Skywalker, Princess Leia, Han Solo, Obi-Wan Kenobi, Darth Vader, C-3PO, R2-D2, Chewbacca, and others exploded on the scene in 1977 and 1978, filling an increasing demand by kids (and adults) to get closer to the characters and "play out" *Star Wars*. With subsequent films came added characters and play sets to create a world worthy of collecting (as referenced in chapter 8). It all had one thing in mind: play *Stars Wars* yourself. Children could fantasize that they were Jedi knights with the Force strong enough to thwart a galactic evil. While the big world can make children feel powerless at times, *Star Wars*—both the films and the toys—helped them imagine what it would be like to be all powerful. It was emotionally *on target*. To put both the *Star Wars* films and merchandise in a broader context, a national news magazine reported in early 1999 that *Star Wars* merchandise raked in approximately $4.5 billion over the first twenty-two years of its existence. This was *four times* as much as the movies. It estimated about *half* was in toys. The toys outsold the film. That, if nothing else, demonstrates the impact that a great story can have upon toys.

Certainly, one-off toys had been made of earlier story icons, most notably from comic books and short-lived televisions shows, but *Star Wars* rocked the industry with a glimpse of what could be. It clearly shows the success that can result when executives develop a great story that's both exciting to "watch" on the big screen and fun to "play" at home.

Lucas ushered in a new era. Studios began to mine the past for stories and invent new ones, looking for solid tales that could support massive franchises. The movie studios began to take the lead because, after all, that's where the stories often started. They learned that crafting a great story must be the priority, because without it, everything else suffers. A great story, with great inspirational characters, well-defined roles, a noble goal, and plenty of great environments and gadgets, makes for blockbuster toys, but only if the story satisfies strong emotional needs to begin with.

The Walt Disney Company has introduced a slew of movies with splendid stories that entertained and oftentimes enlightened, such as *The Lion King, Toy Story, Monsters Inc., Lilo & Stitch,* and many more. Disney created compelling characters that children would want to hold, emulate, and even cuddle. And they did. In the first year of the release of *The Lion King,* sales of toys based on the movie alone surpassed $300 million, according to one source (the film grossed $313 million domestically in 1994). The films fed the Disney Stores with products, the theme parks with products and parades, and the video stores with rentals. But throughout it all, the story and splendid characters are central. "People connect to Disney through our characters and stories," says Matt Ryan, senior vice-president of corporate brand management at The Walt Disney Company. "We try, through our toys and other merchandise, to tap into the emotional connection people feel by making the characters part of their daily lives."

Batman was created in the 1930s by masterful storyteller Bob Kane. It was a sensation for its day, and had all of the right qualities to be successful as both a theatrical release and a toy. It possessed strong characters with strong motivations. It had strong, strange villains. It had unique vehicles, environments, and gadgets. And unlike the more humorous "Batman" television program that appeared in the 1960s, the *Batman* movie created in 1989 was more of a gothic, dark extension of the comic book itself, made possible through the immense talents of the director, Tim Burton. The movie felt strangely real. But Batman had one more element that helped the film and the toys achieve success. It was a franchise that baby-boomer parents knew and loved. It had built-in parent appeal, and so millions of parents flocked to the theater to see the film, almost as excited as the children themselves. It's no wonder then that, after the film's blockbuster success (the first film grossed $251 million domestically), many would-be Batmen asked for, and got, Batman toys. Kids wanted to be the caped crusader, and the movie and the toys helped children fantasize that maybe, just maybe, they would transform into Batman so as to save Gotham City from the likes of the Joker, the Riddler, and Catwoman.

There have been many more success stories of the coalescing of story and toy, with one of the more recent examples being Spider-Man. It's a great tale of a boy who obtains superhuman strength that allows him to soar, swing, suspend, and entangle in order to thwart evil. Boomers flocked to the theater to remember this noble character from their youth. Kids flocked to the theater to be introduced to this noble warrior for justice. The movie grossed a record-shattering $114 million in its opening three-day weekend in May 2002, and over $400 million domestically in 2002. The film served to expand both the audience and the concept of Spider-Man. Al Ovadia, executive vice-president, Sony Pictures Consumer Products, says:

> Entertainment licensing is a multibillion-dollar business that—when it works best—expands the world of the film, the TV show, or the literary asset into tangible items that a casual fan can enjoy and a serious collector can be immersed into in order to understand this world to its fullest. The Spider-Man movie merchandise, like the Spider-Man movie, touched a nerve with the "superhero fan" in all of us. People's imagination was so uniquely satisfied that repeat viewings, along with extensive purchasing and collecting of any and all the Spider-Man merchandise, just kept getting stronger from the release of the movie until well after the DVD/video release, and even remains strong today. We credit this to the filmmakers and our licensing and retail partners, who went above and beyond the normal call of duty in creating a one-of-a-kind entertainment experience and a unique collection of high-quality products. Two of the Spider-Man movie merchandise items that sold the best were the Web Blaster and costume. Both allowed children to experience the world of this character, and expand the story into an adventure in their own backyard.

In fact, the Spider-Man Web Blaster was one of the top blockbuster toys of 2002. Tom McCormack, the VP of research and development at toymaker Toy Biz, a unit of Marvel Enterprises, Inc., told *KidScreen* magazine that it is "the closest we can get to actually shooting a web." The toy allowed the child to pretend to be like Spider-Man as never before, thus enhancing the transformation. The film and the merchandise helped transform children into a noble character they could admire.

The blending of story and toys has been so successful in generating children's smiles that licensed toys derived from movies, books, and so forth can account for a third to a half of all toys sold.

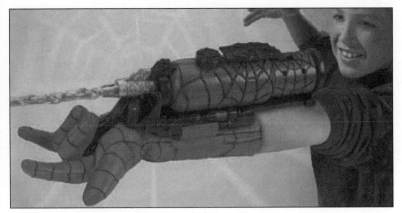

Spider-Man Web Blaster. Courtesy of Marvel, Toy Biz, and Sony.

A Tale of Caution

Though licensing the rights to make toys based upon film or book properties is still critical to the success of many toys today, it's also true the bloom is off the rose. Some toymakers have been severely burned by financial relationships with studios. According to one source, Hasbro guaranteed some $650 million in royalty payments to LucasFilm for the right to produce toys based upon the highly anticipated *Star Wars* prequel, *Episode I: The Phantom Menace.* Hasbro was left with huge inventories that had to be liquidated and significant expenses were written off. But it should be noted that Hasbro sold a lot of toys, for plenty of children asked for and were happy to receive Star Wars playthings, making them a continued blockbuster among children. The problem was that expectations for toy sales were higher than what came to be.

There's a dependence that comes from developing toys based upon a film. The toymaker must depend upon the film being successful, and even if it is, the toymaker must be sure that expectations are kept in line and it does not pay more for the license than it is worth. Because toymakers have been stung, they are becoming more careful. The *Los Angeles Times* reported in April 2002 that "Mattel Inc., the nation's biggest toy maker, cut its licensed toy lines by 25 percent in the past two years, opting to make more original toys instead of weaker film-based games and products." It sounds like a prudent approach, though ignoring studios also increases the odds that the toymaker will miss the Next Big Thing. The smart toymaker looks to create great toys based upon both licensed and original concepts.

Storytelling Toymakers: Where's the Story?

If the toymaker is not licensing a story-based character derived from traditional storytellers (e.g., a studio, book publisher, comic-book publisher, etc.), it is still an important exercise to ask: Where's the story in the toy I am creating? If a story can be woven around the toy, it helps give it focus, personality, and play pattern. Hence, blockbuster toymakers, more than ever, also have to be blockbuster storytellers. It's not always enough to tinker at a bench anymore. Toymakers have to tinker at storytelling. Some toymakers have done so with marvelous results, for whoever invents the story controls the franchise.

The 1981 launch of the Masters of the Universe line proved that toymakers could successfully craft story. The toy line was introduced with a rich tale of a powerful, noble hero (He-Man) whose task was to battle a menacing evil (Skeletor) for control of the entire universe (goal). Introduced at a time when most male action characters were based upon realism (e.g., G.I. Joe), He-Man was a uniquely fresh introduction that reignited the genre. The story gave the characters well-defined roles, equipment, and vehicles. This "story-derived world" drove play pattern, which was heightened by the figures' action features, such as "power punches" created by springlike torsos. The story also allowed the Masters of the Universe to jump into an animated television series and a movie. Hence, the toy gave birth to the entertainment franchise, not the other way around. This was a unique concept in its day.

As a category of toys, video games have been undoubtedly the most successful at weaving stories. Video-game designers discovered early on that their gamer audiences like to live through the story-based characters, overcome great obstacles, and achieve an important goal. While story-based video games were extremely successful, the initial attempts to make movies out of their stories were rocky. The 1993 film debut of the extremely popular Super Mario Bros. game grossed a disappointing $20.9 million at the box office. The 1995 film *Mortal Kombat*, based upon the extremely successful game of the same name, did better at $70 million but was still not considered a blockbuster film. So the question remained as to whether a story derived from a video game was good enough to be a story for the big screen. That, more than anything, would demonstrate that master toymakers could break the category barrier and be master storytellers, too.

The answer came in 2001 with the film debut of *Lara Croft: Tomb Raider,* starring Angelina Jolie and based upon the blockbuster video game that Eidos Interactive created in 1996 for PlayStation. Lara Croft is a sexy, well-armed, and highly capable adventurer in the genre of Indiana Jones. She's tough, beautiful, brave, resourceful, and smart. She gladly launches herself into dangerous situations to fight menacing evils. The story is engaging and the cause noble. In a world in which fictional characters and heroes were predominantly men, Lara is a unique character in a richly unique story. With the aid of master filmmakers, the Tomb Raider story proved truly viable on the big screen. Domestically, the film grossed approximately $48 million on its debut weekend, a record opening for a game-based movie. But it was also a hit by any measure; it was the second highest grossing opening weekend in Paramount's history (behind *Mission Impossible 2*). Its total domestic box office for the year was over $131 million, giving it clear blockbuster status as a film. But more importantly, it proved beyond any doubt that some master toymakers *were* master storytellers.

All toy companies can benefit by realizing that they have potential to be master storytellers and, in so doing, ignite the story lover in the child. That's what led to the success of LEGO's Bionicle, the company's first story-driven universe. A page on the Bionicle Web site begins with, "As the defenders of Ga-Koro faced the Pahrak swarm, it seemed that all would be lost. The village's great monument lay smashed, its buildings torn and tattered, and the Boxors sent to protect it had sunk to the bottom of Lake Naho. . . ." The words trail off, inviting the child to click and read on. The LEGO Company created a story with a full universe of characters and mythology, while using the Internet—among other venues—to convey it. Every six weeks, an update to the site is added so that visitors can explore new areas and enjoy new pieces of the story. And, of course, there are toys that reflect the story, its characters, and the world at large. LEGO has smashed the line that separates toymaker from storyteller, and achieved both sales and much praise from the industry. The story is crafted with such skill that it's not surprising the LEGO Company and Miramax Film have reportedly teamed up to introduce a CGI-animated motion picture based upon the Bionicle series. In many ways, it demonstrates that toymakers should first be storytellers because, more and more, the story must precede the toy in order to ensure that the right foundation is set for the introduction of the playthings.

Any toy can benefit from storytelling. Beyblade toys are high-performance tops that kids can custom make. In fact, they are sold unassembled for that very purpose, and children can mix and match parts from other Beyblade tops to achieve their desired configuration. That's special because it gives the child the ability to mold it to their own tastes, much like the Build-A-Bear concept cited in chapter 7, putting Beyblade *on emotional target* while using technology that places it *on trend*. But in addition, Beyblades are wrapped in a story of good and evil, of heroes and monsters, with the centerpiece being the

Beystadium, where the tops (as characters) battle for supremacy. The last character spinning is the champion. It's a fascinating example of a basic toy (a top) that has been with humankind for thousands of years, virtually unchanged, made suddenly special and more intriguing with the addition of a story-based play pattern. That story lent itself to animated entertainment, which in turn gave greater emotional depth and excitement to the toy.

More than ever, toymakers must also be storytellers. It doesn't matter if, as a toymaker, you are developing a new video game, doll, male action line, ball, skateboard, or yo-yo. Just ask yourself this: What's the compelling story we can weave to enhance the toy through multidimensional characters, noble goals, and rich environments? How can we transform the child into a story lover? The more compelling the story, the more likely you will have not only a blockbuster toy but also a blockbuster piece of entertainment that can jump to books, film, video, and parades. It will give you the opportunity to bring joy to children in ways you never imagined that your yo-yo or ball could ever achieve by itself.

The Next Big Thing: Basic Principles

• Look for great upcoming stories produced by others, but think of yourself as a storyteller, too.

• Invent stories that can imbue toys with greater meaning so that children can reach greater levels of emotional fulfillment. Craft those stories with relatable, unique characters that possess noble goals. Create rich environments. Convey that story either in the context of your own toy (e.g., video games) or in the broader media and marketing context (e.g., advertising, Web sites, even printed panels on packaging).

CHAPTER 10

Create an Experience Seeker

Toys began their journey in a very one-dimensional way. The earliest of toys such as kites and yo-yos often did one thing, such as fulfilling a very narrow, task-based need often related to mastery (e.g., get the kite up into the air, get the yo-yo to return). These were very fun tasks and have remained so for ages. The fun derived from involvement in a simple task would apply to many other ancient and contemporary blockbuster toys. For many years, for instance, a multitude of children have taken delight in making the Slinky (1945) walk downstairs. The fun of making it—and watching it—slink about helped make it become a blockbuster toy.

As time progressed, toys began to expand beyond single-focused, one-dimensional activities and began to satisfy more intricate human needs. The game of Monopoly makes us feel rich, the Barbie doll allows girls to touch endless aspirations, and Erector Sets and LEGO building bricks allow kids to become creators. Even the blockbuster View-Master 3D Virtual Viewer, launched in 1939, eventually began taking children on visual adventures to places they had never been but wished they could go. When the toy was packed with images of Disney characters—and particularly images of the new Disneyland amusement park in the 1950s—View-Master sales skyrocketed. The View-Master was, in effect, selling fantasies. Such advancements in toys were significant milestones because they meant that a child's greater emotional needs were being recognized. Toymakers began developing playthings to satisfy those more intricate needs, thus breaking into what I call the second dimension.

Some toys added a third dimension, this being *the story* as referenced in the last chapter. This not only created a platform for the other dimensions (task-based play and deeper emotional drivers), but it allowed toys to take on greater personality and provided roles for the child. This is most clearly demonstrated in the past several decades with the rise in importance of the Hollywood studio in the making of toys. Through wonderful storytelling, films like *Star Wars* created a foundation that brought life to characters and environments, which translated very well into playthings.

The Fourth Dimension: The Total Experience

The industry is now at the gate of the fourth dimension, and its awesome power is beginning to be felt. In the past several years, some toys and games have scratched the surface of a new form of engagement: providing a full, multidimensional, role-playing experience. There's no better example of this than video games.

In an earlier chapter, I noted that video-game developers often create a story, and that this story gives life and personality to the characters. But video games do more than that. They give children—and adults—control on an unprecedented scale. Blockbuster video games don't just allow gamers to play the games; *they allow them to enter the games*. Gamers decide which car to drive or which character to emulate. They decide whether they should run down this corridor or the other to thwart evil and save the world. They decide whether they should take the hoop shot or toss it to a buddy closer to the basket. The realism brought to the video-game environment through graphics and sounds heightens the enjoyment because it heightens the fantasy. The platform helps satisfy the emotional drivers outlined in chapter 2 as never before. Kids today seek not just play, but experiences.

Compare this to the real world, in which children have so little control over their day. The decisions a child faces are not often made by them, or if they are, they are heavily influenced by others. Children are often told when to get up in the morning, what to eat for breakfast, and so on. It's no wonder, then, that video games offer something that a child's real world cannot: a chance to be in control and be a hero in ways that the real world will not allow. Whereas a toy based upon a movie will entice a child to play and even emulate a character, a blockbuster video game allows the child to more readily take on the role of that character, make decisions like that character might make, and then win or lose because of the child's own decisions. And if the child does lose, they have only to begin again and make a different set of decisions until the outcome puts them in the winner's circle. Great video games offer a multidimensional experience that allows children to safely experience and "try on" a new life like no other toy has to date. Children can do such in the privacy of their rooms, where the controlling world on the outside is not allowed in, and where the child gets to be the ultimate decider of their own destiny.

Blockbuster video games tap into all of the elements in toys and games that came before—the basic tasks of the first dimension, the deeper emotional drivers that constituted the second dimension, the story that brought toys and games to the third dimension—yet now with the added, immense control and realism of the fourth dimension. Combined, it's a massive multidimensional experience that places video games *on emotional target* in ways that no plaything was able to achieve before. In this way, blockbuster video games tap into that part of every child—and every adult gamer—that wants a thrilling experience not typically available. Blockbuster video games pull the experience seeker in all of us to the surface.

The history of the video game is an interesting one, as it

demonstrates that it went through the basic four dimensions, though rather quickly by historical standards. It began in the 1970s when Atari, founded by Nolan Bushnell, introduced a home version of Pong, a very simple, one-dimensional game where players bounced a ball back and forth across a court on their television screen. It fulfilled a basic need for simple mastery and competition. It sounds like a yawn now, but it created a tidal wave in the toy world, not so much for the game as for the potential. The category expanded into two dimensions (greater emotional rewards) when games such as Space Invaders were introduced around 1980. The Space Invaders cartridge for the Atari made over $100 million, which is a huge sum even today, making it a blockbuster. The potential for games to provide emotional fulfillment was expanded further

Atari 2600 circa 1977. From the author's personal collection.

with the 1979 introduction of another blockbuster game system, Mattel's Intellivision. It added far more realistic graphics and sounds. Intellivision's Major League Baseball game sold a million copies. Its Night Stalker game, about a man trying to survive various beasts, was a huge success as well. And it demonstrated that the themes and emotional drivers the toymakers attempted to fulfill were expanding ever so slightly into story (the third dimension), while providing for greater control in a multidimensional experience (the fourth dimension). Most of these games, however, did not have a rich, sweeping story or the kind of challenge and control that would keep kids coming back day after day. And so the market for video games suddenly evaporated. While industry sales were reportedly $3 billion in 1981, they crashed to about $100 million by 1983. There were too many products flooding the market and not enough benefits sustaining consumers' interest. It was devastating for the industry. All of the leading video-game companies left the business.

Nintendo Showed the Way

Enter Nintendo, a mere year or so later. The birth of today's robust video-game market can be traced to New York in late 1985 when Nintendo test marketed the Nintendo Entertainment System (NES) in the United States. Based upon the encouraging results, NES was launched nationwide the following year. Results were spectacular, which was counterintuitive at the time because the video-game market was still reeling from its very painful collapse. Then what, exactly, accounted for the success of NES?

One particular game developed for NES created an enticing story that engaged children by tapping into their desire to seek an exciting experience. The story allowed children to "enter" it by taking on the role and controlling the actions of a tiny hero plumber named Mario (Super Mario Bros.). This character danced around one deadly hurdle after another (with the child's aid) to achieve a noble goal (save the princess). Evil was lurking around every corner, but with persistence, a child could beat each of the eight levels, master the game, vanquish all the bad guys, and save Princess Toadstool. The game was delicately balanced—not so hard that it defied being won nor so easy that it could be solved too fast. It was an achievable challenge, level for level, until the grand goal was reached. Nintendo arrived at the fourth dimension. It was not just a game and not just a story; it was a multidimensional experience filled with challenge after challenge. It was an adventure and in many ways it was an escape. The NES eight-bit processor added mightily to the graphics to make the adventure and experience come alive more than previous video games had. It placed the platform *on trend* by using more powerful technology to satisfy a child's desire for a greater sensory experience.

NES was a blockbuster toy, not only because it was a huge financial success, not only because it triumphed at a time when everyone thought the market was dead, and not only because it enticed millions of children to smile, but because it paved the way for a new generation of playthings. Nintendo followed Super Mario Bros. with a slew of other blockbuster games, such as the wildly successful Legend of Zelda. Each successful game allowed Nintendo to remain at the forefront of the industry and cool with its audiences (*regenerative*). But at the heart of each of these games was the story, the control and escape it offered, the challenge it provided, and the multidimensional sensory experience that brought it to life. Nintendo showed the entire toy and gaming world how to do it right. By 1990, it was estimated that NES was in one of every three homes in the United States.

Other video-game manufacturers took the cue and the race was on to provide the right combination of story, control, and realism (typically a function of graphics and sound based upon the power of the CPU). To this day, manufacturers such as Sony (PlayStation) and Microsoft (Xbox) compete with

Nintendo's newest generation of games (GameCube) to supply the most robust experience. But the role Nintendo played, and continues to play, has earned it blockbuster status again and again. Nintendo even brought that experience to the handheld video-game platform in its highly successful Game Boy line, referenced in an earlier chapter.

Though I have spoken much of video games, one cannot ignore the computer as a platform for some of the most amazing, blockbuster games that have transformed children and adults alike into experience seekers. One particular blockbuster, Myst, took the market by surprise in 1993. The game virtually drops the player in a foreign, intricately beautiful world and, with no instructions, challenges the player to unravel puzzle after puzzle to help save the world and vanquish those whose aim is to destroy it. It was—and is—utterly breathtaking in story, graphics, and scope. It became the best-selling PC game ever, with over 10 million units sold (which includes the original Myst and the two sequels). Myst proved, beyond any doubt, the power of creating a full, robust experience, made possible at the time by the power of the computer chip. The more real the experience and adventure and the better the storytelling, the more likely it is that the child—and adult—will connect emotionally with the toy or game. But the makers of Myst had a challenge, and that was how to follow it up with a powerful sequel that would expand the experience.

Ken Goldstein, former vice-president and executive publisher at Broderbund Software, says:

> Contrary to otherwise cynical exploitation, a good sequel is a very difficult thing to do. The immense pressure on a creative team to follow up a hit with another hit building on similar subject matter weighs heavily on all involved. Indeed, the ability to repeat success can be the difference between a one-off win and the creation of an enduring brand; fail, and you destroy the legacy of your previous achievement. When the creators of Myst set out to develop Riven, the sequel to Myst, they knew what was

fundamentally at stake, that the expectations of their loyal enthusiasts demanded not a replay of the original, but the absolute expansion of its vision. *Myst created a world; Riven had to prove that this world was boundless.* In meeting that challenge, Cyan took Myst from renowned game to timeless brand, opening the door as wide as they could to future possibilities. Handled correctly, a sequel is an awesome responsibility, a challenge, and an opportunity to exceed an audience's expectations, transcend the status of fad, and become etched in popular culture. Perhaps that is why Myst as a brand remains a benchmark of creative quality, because its creators never let it become anything less.

Riven created a richly intricate experience that built mightily upon Myst and, in so doing, became a blockbuster sequel.

A Glimpse at the Potential

The search for a multidimensional experience is not over, not by a long shot. The trek continues with EverQuest, a blockbuster online multiplayer game where almost half a million players meet in cyberspace. Each player takes on the role of a character by choosing from among fourteen races and fifteen classes, including dwarves, ogres, and wizards. Across five enormous continents, they can meet other characters, form alliance guilds, and battle monsters . . . either alone or by working together. Players, who have never met in life and live thousands of miles apart in our world, are suddenly bound side by side on great adventures (the average age is thirty-one). This is the near future of video games, which is why manufacturers are racing to add online components to their products. EverQuest is an immersion into a world where, in disguise, you can meet other humans who are similarly disguised. In many respects, it's a play, and each player is part of the cast. The story unfolds solely by the decisions you, the player, make. With EverQuest, the player has a virtual life. The fact that EverQuest is under the auspices of Sony indicates the importance that entertainment companies place on this emerging medium.

Screenshot of EverQuest® II—used with permission of Sony Online Entertainment. EverQuest is a registered trademark of Sony Computer Entertainment America Inc. in the U.S. and/or other countries. © 2003 Sony Computer Entertainment America Inc. All rights reserved.

The Walt Disney Internet Group is introducing a new multiplayer online game called Disney's Toontown Online, where children can create and then become a toon character, meet other toon characters, and pretend to live in a fun toon world. The fact that Disney understands the excitement this format can bring to children (when done in a way that reflects the audience's younger age) and is able to keep the community safe bodes well for the future of online games. "Walt Disney created the modern theme park," says Ken Goldstein, who is now the executive vice-president and managing director of Disney Online. "Our goal is to create the online theme park. Walt was a pioneer in everything he pursued—short-subject animation, theatrical-feature animation, live-action family motion pictures, documentaries, television series, live attractions—but the one medium he never got to explore was the personal computer and its unending offshoots. We aim to take forward his creative vision, his respect for technology, and his mission to make entertainment magical into a virtual but equally engaging environment, where kids and their parents can safely connect with others to play, to learn, and to explore."

As users become familiar with these greater experiences and sensations, their expectations rise, and manufacturers must ensure that multiplayer games deliver. This was a caution experienced by the introduction of the Sims Online, based upon the highly successful Sims game by Electronic Arts Inc. The online version allows thousands of people to live virtual lives by meeting others online, building businesses, and even getting married. But soon after the introduction, a headline in the *Los Angeles Times* read, "Sims Online Gives Creators a Painful Reality Check." It went on to report that many consumers were disappointed by the online version of the game, saying that it was "shallow . . . pointless . . . tedious." Still, success will be had by those that get it right, either initially or over time as they fine tune their offerings.

The PC and video-game environments have become such powerful platforms that youth have been unwilling to leave video games behind as they age. One report claims that 57 percent of all console games are played by adults over eighteen, as are 70 percent of PC-based games. As a category, this new form of electronic pastime (on a video-game console or computer) has become a truly new platform of entertainment, surpassing even movies in revenue. The total 2001 U.S. dollar sales of the

"Interactive Entertainment Industry" were approximately $10.5 billion. In 2002, sales were expected to top $12 billion. This includes video- and computer-game software, consoles, and handhelds. In comparison, the 2001 U.S. movie box office was approximately $8.4 billion. Electronic entertainment outsells movies. It is interesting to note that more and more studios are now taking their cue from the gaming industry. Lara Croft: Tomb Raider, mentioned in the last chapter, demonstrated the opportunity that can be fulfilled when the right game is brought into the theaters. It also demonstrates that the power may be gradually shifting, away from those who own the story and toward those who own the *multidimensional story experience*.

Yet, the video- and computer-game industry is still in its infancy. Many schools across the United States provide degrees in film, but only a handful provide a degree in game art and design. Until the industry grows its own, it will not be as great a force as it could be. The Art Institute of California at Los Angeles is at the forefront of change. It offers a bachelor's degree of science in game art and design. By scanning the curriculum, you can see the immense potential of the program; it includes classes in storytelling, animation, game-level design, 3-D modeling, and psychology. Dave Moughalian, dean of education at the college, says, "Our game art and design degree is a hybrid program: a combination of broad-based cultural dialog joined with technical and design skills, enabling the student to fully develop the means to create their own interactive story experience." In effect, the graduates are being prepared to create games that achieve the fourth dimension. These graduates will be the first in wave after wave that will follow them. When these waves hit the marketplace, the entertainment industry will be transformed as new generations of playthings achieve the fourth dimension in ways that we cannot even imagine today. We have seen nothing yet.

Where is all this heading? Some manufacturers intend to

add even greater sensory experiences, such as computers that emit fragrances to match the players' environment. As an adventurer walks through a bed of roses, for example, the computer will produce a rose fragrance. If an adventurer meets a foul-smelling troll, well, you can imagine. Some arcade games provide virtual-reality experiences where families can ride a river raft down rapids or fight invaders that appear on the visors of virtual-reality helmets. Those experiences, however, are a small fragment of the possibilities. The endgame, as technology allows, is best represented in the Holodeck concept of *Star Trek*, where a player would enter a room that emits holographic images of lifelike people, environments, and adventures. Gamers will be able to experience real-life thrills, risks, adventures, and challenges. The video games that best offer the next leap in multidimensional experiences and realistic adventures, while affording experience seekers ultimate control, will dominate. They will be *on emotional target, on trend,* and *regenerative*. Why watch a movie when you can live it? Why pretend to emulate a doll when you can experience what it's like to live the life of that character?

Having mentioned the future, it's important to note that there are many more traditional toys that have become blockbusters because they added a modest experiential component in their day. The Operation Skill Game is a blockbuster. It allows children to *feel* more like real doctors by operating on a pretend patient, and harming the patient on occasion if their surgery wasn't precise enough. Monopoly, as we discussed earlier, allows game players to *feel* more like real millionaires. Cabbage Patch Kids allow girls to *feel* more like real moms. But as even traditional toys better use technology to insert story, to provide greater player control, and to offer more realistic adventures, they will have a greater opportunity to break into the fourth dimension as well, thus transforming themselves into the world's new breed of blockbusters.

The Next Big Thing: Basic Principles

• Invent toys that provide a multidimensional experience for the child (and adult).

• Transform participants into seekers of an experience, as real as it can be (safely), so that they truly *feel* and *participate* in the adventure and the fantasy.

• Review even the most common toys to ascertain if you can add more experiential components, thus heightening interest.

CHAPTER 11

Create a Plaything in Everything

Many marketers of children's products have a silo mentality: food is food, a beverage is a beverage, a pencil is a pencil, candy is candy, a basketball is a basketball, a movie is a movie, and toys are toys. They often work in one of these categories for many years and seldom review other categories as in-depth as they might. They read the journals about their specific industry, say sporting goods, conduct research on specific products they are introducing, talk to the industry gurus who have worked in the category for years, and pay little attention to what's going on elsewhere. As a result, they don't always see interesting elements of one category that have the potential to be brought into their category. Years of industry convention influence them to define their industry in a very narrow context.

Because they have not been indoctrinated by industry convention and years of acculturation, children easily blur the lines between what is a toy and what is a food, a pencil, a T-shirt, and so forth. They see the potential for playthings in all things. They readily accept, and desire to have, toylike qualities infused into that food, pencil, and T-shirt. Even products as common as a beverage have the potential to transform children into masters, creators, nurturers, emulators, friends, collectors, story lovers, and experience seekers, thus fulfilling needs for such emotional drivers as power, control, silliness, and independence. We mentioned in an earlier chapter that

in the past few decades the walls between at least two categories—toymaking and storytelling—have collapsed, and busi-
nesspeople have realized that children are willing and able to
appreciate each as an extension of the other. But the potential
is far greater.

Master toymakers have a great opportunity to bring their
skills to every single product consumed by children so as to
create blockbuster playthings in all guises and product types.
In fact, toymakers should not even define their category as *toys*,
per se, for doing so limits possibilities.

Seeds of Play

Some pioneers in children's products recognized this early on
and took steps to introduce toylike elements in their products.
One of the earliest efforts to do so on a national scope came
from an unlikely source, a molasses-covered popcorn morsel.
The first such product was actually created by early New England
Indian tribes, but it was introduced commercially by F. W.
Rueckheim at Chicago's first World Fair in 1893. The product
achieved some prominence in the early 1900s but was celebrated
in a grand way when featured in the words of an immortal 1908
song called "Take Me Out to the Ball Game." When baseball *was*
the one true national pastime and every kid in every town across
America wanted to be a professional baseball player, the nation
huddled around the baseball diamond or the radio and sang the
words, "Buy me some peanuts and Cracker Jack. . . ." Cracker
Jack Caramel Coated Popcorn & Peanuts became a piece of
America and remains so to this day. It was associated with baseball when baseball was at its peak, placing in *on trend*.

But it was in 1912 when something seemingly trivial, but
with widespread implications, happened to Cracker Jack. It
added "a prize in every box." It was one of the first of its kind,
a packaged-good brand that included playthings. While this
might seem very commonplace today, in the early 1900s it was
a revolution. "A Prize in Every Box" became as much a part of

Vintage Cracker Jack box. From the author's personal collection.

the Cracker Jack brand as was the caramel treat inside. While the caramel treat satisfied the sweet tooth, the toy allowed the brand to satisfy an array of emotional drivers, subject only to the nature of the toy itself. That helped Cracker Jack be highly *on emotional target.* Cracker Jack playthings have included puzzles, tattoos, dolls, games, tricks, charms, tops, rings, stickers, marbles, spinners, whistles, a magnifying glass, and many more. Each new prize made Cracker Jack new again and again, connecting with different emotional drivers and allowing the brand to be highly *regenerative* each year. Children would look forward to the next surprise, which created a lasting sense of anticipation. Since 1912, more than 17 billion playthings have come in Cracker Jack boxes. Today, more than 100 million toy prizes are distributed each year. Cracker Jack is not just a blockbuster snack, it's a blockbuster plaything. The business model it created was adopted by many other manufacturers and continues to this very day.

McDonald's took this concept to a new level in 1977 with the successful test of the first Happy Meal in Kansas City. It was introduced in 1978 with a circus wagon theme. As the world knows, the Happy Meal offers food packaged with a plaything, such as a toy, puzzles, or games of various sorts. The Happy Meal has included themes from films (e.g., Bambi Happy Meal), toys (e.g., Hot Wheels Happy Meal), sporting events (e.g., Olympic Sports Happy Meal), regional theme parks (e.g., Sea World Happy Meal), and many more. Similar to Cracker Jack, the Happy Meal has allowed McDonald's to stay *on trend, on many emotional targets,* and highly *regenerative.* To this day, when children ask for a Happy Meal, they are probably asking as much for the toy item that's inside as they are for the food. The Happy Meal became not only a blockbuster meal but a blockbuster plaything. It's a product that allows McDonald's to remain Ever-Cool with kids because Happy Meals are associated with whatever themes or fads are popular at the time, from movies and television shows to toys and theme parks. More than 20 percent of McDonald's transactions in the U.S. are reportedly due to the Happy Meal, which comes to about $3.5 billion in annual revenue. That does not account for the adult meals the restaurant sells to parents who accompany their children on a Happy Meal quest.

Blurring Categories

Still, in both the Cracker Jack and Happy Meal examples, it is clear that the plaything and the food are separate entities. The toys and games are used as sales promotions and premiums to help sell the food. The brand that began to truly blur this distinction was first introduced in 1927 in Austria as a peppermint for adult smokers. When it was launched in America in 1952, it was reformulated to appeal to kids' tastes and came in dispensers with brightly colored character heads. Just tilt the head back and the candy pops out. The brand, of course, is PEZ Candy. Is it a candy or a toy? It is both. It perfectly blends the qualities of each. Since its introduction, PEZ Candy has created over 250 character heads, many of which reflect favorite characters from silly cartoon figures to superheroes to holiday characters. Recently, PEZ Candy has expanded its line to include an amazing array of toylike designs. It offers candy-dispensing toy cars, pens, and telephones. The brand also offers "body parts" that a child can use to dress up a PEZ Candy dispenser. The suits include a knight, spaceman, jungle man, nurse, and cowgirl. Once PEZ began offering other toylike features and dressing up its dispensers, it greatly expanded the emotional needs the brand can satisfy. PEZ Candy demonstrated that playthings and foods can merge, that in so doing many emotional drivers can be satisfied, and that children would not only accept it but truly appreciate it when ordinary items in their world suddenly take on the properties of toys. Over 3 billion PEZ Candies are consumed each year in the U.S. It's a blockbuster candy-toy.

PEZ Candy dispensers. From the author's personal collection.

The cereal to provide a sound was, of course, Kellogg's Rice Krispies cereal. It went "Snap! Crackle! Pop!" It had, and has, a wonderful playable quality to it. Imagine a child growing up in a world of do-nothing cereals and suddenly *hearing* this one make a racket. Such experiences can make a lasting impression.

But it still took years before other manufacturers provided playable qualities. The basic idea behind Pop Rocks candy was patented by General Foods in the 1960s and introduced in 1976. As we know, it's the candy that fizzes and pops when tossed into the mouth. The Easy-Bake Oven (1963) is one of the few blockbuster concepts that bridged the gap between a toy and a food. It demonstrated what can be. Amurol Confections Company introduced a variety of candies and gums that have playable qualities and themes. They include Bubble Tape Bubble Gum, Squeeze Pop Liquid Lollipops, Bug City, Thumb Suckers, and Bubble Beeper. Their approach reflected the PEZ Candy business model: sell a candylike treat inside a fun contemporary container.

But it wasn't until the mid-1990s and onward that a slew of other items began to sweep across the marketplace. Cheetos Mystery Colorz tint a child's tongue blue or green. A variety of the Kool-Aid Magic Twists product begins as a green powder, changes to blue, but tastes like cherry. Such brands turn children into experience seekers. Quaker Oatmeal Treasure Hunt includes brown chests that turn into the colors and shapes of emeralds and rubies when hot water is added. It can help transform children into fanciful millionaires, if only during breakfast. Heinz E-Z Squirt is ketchup that comes in green and purple varieties. Kids can use it to "decorate" their hot dogs and hamburgers. It helps transform children into fun artists and creators using a new medium, their food. All of these items help create a playable experience for the child, in addition to their more conventional category traits (taste appeal).

When does a book become a toy, or a toy a book? That

question was answered with the introduction of a 1977 book entitled *Juggling for the Complete Klutz,* which was a how-to book (with juggling cubes) for those who were juggling challenged. From the very beginning, Klutz books were "designed for doing, not just reading." This has expanded into a book line that contains over 150 titles, including how-to books for *Beaded Bobby Pins* (how to make stylish hair ornaments), *The Body Crayon Book* (how to turn your body into a canvas for art), and even *Eat This Book* (how to have fun writing on, and eating, twenty edible pages). Klutz has sold over 60 million books around the world, making it a blockbuster, playable book franchise. Today, many other publishers have taken notice, particularly in the preschool category, and have introduced a wide range of books with do-something, toylike features.

What Does It Do?

Toys in the 1980s began to add numerous mechanical features, so much so that when children were shown a new product concept even for the simplest toys, the first question they often asked was, what does it do? I remember those days very well. If the toy did not "do something" special over and above what other toys did, the concept oftentimes failed (the original Cabbage Patch Kids was a wonderful exception because it avoided the technology that sometimes got in the way of the emotional connection). Still, children's expectations were growing higher, often because children had the capacity for more "do something" products and because manufacturers started to raise the bar in order to distinguish their toys from the others. More and more, I have begun to hear children raise the same question in other nontoy categories: what does it do? That applies to foods, beverages, apparel, and more. "What does it do?" is a question all manufacturers must ask themselves, most notably because children are asking for toylike properties in all things.

By answering the "what does it do?" question, a brand can

help satisfy strong emotional drivers beyond what's traditional in a given category. L.A. Gear created a sensation with the introduction of L.A. Lights athletic shoes, which came with lights embedded in their soles. They blinked when the child walked. This is commonplace now, but when they were introduced it was a true phenomenon. Children who wore them drew fun attention and felt special as a result. Street Flyer Retractable In-Line Skates by Street Flyer Inc. are sneakers that come with skates embedded in the soles. The wheels flip up or down as desired. "Why walk when you can fly?" says the company's slogan. These shoes have a secret, which can make the child feel special for knowing the secret. The shoes help kids suddenly put on some speed, which can make them feel empowered. The shoes are highly visible as the child zips in and out of foot traffic, which can help them be the center of attention, if only for a moment. The brand turns children from walkers into flyers at a moment's notice, and from mere pedestrians to road warriors.

The answer to the question of "what does it do?" can often be found in common things in one industry applied to another industry where it is not common. Apply the common alphabet to a food product and you might obtain Alpha-Bits cereal. The Web site for the brand states, "Only Alpha-Bits has 26 tasty little letters in every bowl to spark kids' imaginations in a way that no other cereal can. So breakfast is a new experience each and every day." The brand helps children learn and explore the alphabet. It can help transform children into masters and adventurers in fun, subtle ways. Yoplait turned a common adult food into an uncommon child's food by introducing Go-Gurt portable yogurt. It comes in a tube that children can eat (slurp!) on the go. Given children's rather crunched schedules these days and their desire for playable foods, Go-Gurt is highly *on trend*. A version of Fun Fruits Fruit Snacks comes in the shape of checkers so that children can play with the snacks before they eat them.

The point of all this is simple. Toymakers should never be restricted in their thinking to the traditional definition of toys or even the toy category. They should think of themselves as *playmakers* with the ability to bring play to all categories. Similarly, nontoymakers need to think more broadly and should consider adding toylike qualities to their products. Can your nontoy product offer a sound, a sight, a different feel/touch, a fragrance, or a taste experience? Can you take a common element in the toy category and apply it to your category in an interesting way? Where is the whole-wheat bread that makes a sound? Where is the peanut butter that's green? Where is the skateboard that's also a boom box? Where are the cookies shaped like characters that battle for supreme control of the universe? Where is the toy that dispenses a beverage? Where is the male action toy line that dispenses candies?

Experimenting with the answers to these questions can help the toymaker invent new playable products. The truth is that the Next Big Thing in toys may not look like a toy at all, at least not in the standard definition of toys. That's because children have the capacity and desire to have playthings in all things. This is not just about supplying generic "fun." It is about satisfying strong emotional drivers in categories that currently satisfy only a small portion of their full potential. You can help children transform as much with a cookie as you can with a toy. To be a blockbuster toymaker today means that you must think of the toy category as only one of many canvases upon which you can create the next blockbuster plaything.

The Next Big Thing: Basic Principles

• Toymakers need to think of themselves as playmakers and never confine themselves to the traditional definition of toys. Nontoymakers should think of themselves as toymakers and strive to add elements of play to their products.

• A simple approach is to offer toy premiums in nontoy products (e.g., the Cracker Jack approach).

- Try to blur categories by more closely combining toylike properties with other categories that children enjoy (e.g., PEZ Candy).
- Look to gratify a child's senses via sights, sounds, and so forth in categories and products that are currently plain and generic (e.g., green Heinz E-Z Squirt).
- Take common elements from one category and apply them to others where it is novel (e.g., Alpha-Bits cereal).
- Take adult products and reinvent them in safe, kid-friendly ways (e.g., Go-Gurt yogurt).
- Ask of your new product: what does it do?

Chapter 12

Blockbuster Marketing

Whereas the previous chapters of this book focused primarily upon the core elements to help the child transform (being *on emotional target* with the child, being *on emotional target* with the parent, being *on trend* in the greater society, and being *regenerative*), the following chapters will concentrate primarily on the remaining two contributors (i.e., *playful marketing* and the *X Factor*—defined as the unpredictable, serendipitous moment).

In today's sophisticated world, it's not enough for professionals to be strictly toymakers, tinkering at a bench with a new contraption. Competition to inspire a child's request and a parent's purchase intent is immense, and the marketing dollars spent are formidable. Today's toymakers must also be toy marketers. Even if you work in your garage and are a solo inventor, you must think about how to market your product in a fun and playful way. If you do not, you may have a toy with potential that never makes it into the honored blockbuster realm. Any would-be toymakers should ask themselves a few basic questions, such as: Does my new toy idea strongly satisfy deep emotional needs in the child and/or parent? Is my new toy unique? Does its uniqueness make a real difference? Beyond these fundamental considerations, toymakers must ask additional questions that will have considerable impact on marketing and promotion plans:

• Does my new toy have such a unique perspective that it will be newsworthy?

179

• Does my new toy have something about it that will easily lead to great, playful advertising?

• Does my new toy have something about it that will easily lead to great, playful promotions, either alone or with other manufacturers?

• Does my new toy have something about it that will excite the trade and build foot traffic in stores?

• Is my new toy conducive to unique distribution avenues such as direct marketing via mail, catalog, etc.?

If toymakers consider these issues as the toy is still under development, they will have the opportunity to alter the design of the toy itself in ways that will help it to achieve blockbuster status. I have seen it happen in countless meetings. The toy ideas that often get sold to upper management are not necessarily those that have the most playful features, per se, but those that inspire the best, *playful marketing*. When executives hover over a toy that is the most "marketable," they begin to spontaneously and effortlessly generate ideas for playful public relations, playful advertising, playful consumer promotions, and playful trade promotions. They can "see" a very exciting marketing plan. Toys that do not lend themselves to these initiatives are a harder sell. It's not that they do not have the potential to excite kids, but they don't have the potential to excite marketing, which is the vehicle executives use to gain attention from the trade, children, and parents.

A Toy with a Plan

Successful blockbuster marketing entails having an understanding of the key marketing elements. A simple—and general—approach is in exhibit 2. It depicts the key marketing disciplines and the role each might play in creating awareness, interest, and purchase of a specific toy. Public relations often begin before the other disciplines. Its objective, in general, is to help generate initial interest and excitement. Advertising generates added awareness and interest but also trial and

Exhibit 2
Blockbuster Marketing Elements!

Communication Discipline	Pre-Sale				Post-Sale			
	Create Awareness	Interest	Trial	Purchase	Usage	Support	Satisfaction	Added Purchases
Public Relations	X	X						
Advertising	X	X	X	X				X
In Store Materials		X	X	X				X
Packaging		X	X	X				X
Promotions		X	X	X				X
Direct Marketing		X	X	X				X
Call Centers					X	X	X	

eventual purchase. In-store materials and packaging also generate interest, trial, and purchase, as do promotions and direct marketing. Call centers help address consumer needs after purchase to help with toys that might need added explanation or service. Many of these disciplines help create repeat purchase. The objectives of the marketing elements in this exhibit are very general, however. Specific objectives will vary from toy to toy. American Girl Dolls rely on direct-marketing catalogs to help generate awareness and interest. Some public relations efforts have proven so powerful that they led to immense sales. New media venues such as the online environment cross all of these communication disciplines and have great potential for developing a positive relationship with children, when handled in ways that parents approve of.

The point of this basic structure is simple: to help toymakers, at the earliest point possible, begin to think through the marketing plan even as the toy is still under development. The more that you can "see" the marketing implications of the toy concept, the more you will be able to adjust the toy's design to help inspire great, playful marketing. That will greatly help the toymaker—designer—sell ideas to upper management, to marketers, and to the consumer.

This does not mean, by the way, that the best-*marketed* toys are not necessarily the best toys. But if two toys equally fulfill emotional needs, the one that will succeed is that which can also inspire fun, playful marketing. In the ideation workshops I run for clients, I often divide the day into two parts. The first part is used to generate product concepts based upon child or parent needs, trends, and so forth. Once we have the initial ideas, the second part of the session is devoted to generating marketing ideas for each toy concept. That simple procedure tells us which toy concepts have the greatest potential. Two concepts may look equally strong in step one (being *on emotional target* and being *on trend*), but it is a very common occurrence in step two that one concept suddenly outshines the other, based upon the depth and breadth of playful marketing ideas that spontaneously spring from it.

The following chapters are the key marketing elements that the toymaker must consider, including public relations, advertising, promotions, and packaging. The big toy manufacturers have each of these disciplines at their disposal. But the solo toymaker in his or her garage, and even the toymaker in a large toy company, will be better able to sell their ideas if they better understand how other executives will evaluate them. As no time previously, the best toymakers are those who also have insights into the big marketing picture. This will help the toymaker not only generate a new, fun toy idea but an idea with a solid, playful plan to make it a blockbuster.

The Audience

A critical decision will be the selection of the audience for marketing communications. Are the various marketing communications going to speak to parents alone, children alone, or both? The influence curve in exhibit 3 helps to answer this question. It shows how dramatically child influence increases as the children get older. The amount of influence they exercise is an important factor, but only one factor, to help the toymaker decide whom the communications should be directed toward. By the time a child reaches age eight to ten, as much as 70 percent of the toys they receive are a function of direct or indirect child requests. Because of this, a general guideline is that when children are five years old and older, it's more important to communicate directly to them due to their increased influence in the home. If the child is age four or younger, communications are more often directed primarily toward the parents because the child is not as influential. A two-year-old child, for example, does not make as many requests as a five-year-old, and the requests they make are not well prioritized. By the time a child reaches ages five and older, they are apt to make far more requests, and they are

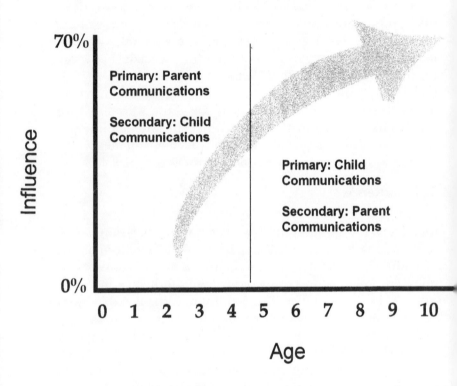

Exhibit 3
Influence Curve

much better at prioritizing requests. And for every toy they ask for, they are not asking for hundreds of others that will, as a result, fail in the marketplace. That makes children's influence great at those older ages and less so at younger ages. Given the child's more tender ages of four and below, it is often best that the parent be addressed directly, anyway.

This does not mean that parental communications are unimportant for the older child. While advertising may generate awareness of a toy among these older children, and be the primary means of communication overall, the package becomes an important tool to communicate to parents the toy's benefits, contents, and age appropriateness to help the parent decide if the toy is suitable for their child. It's vital that the parent be given adequate knowledge about the toy to help them decide. Does this mean that child communication is unimportant for the younger child? No. While advertising may be directed to parents, elements such as colors and characters that appeal to the younger child may be prominently displayed on the package or the product so that the child and parents know that this item has the child's preferences in mind. In this way, the total communications plan needs to speak to multiple audiences in ways that are meaningful to each, while balancing the primary and secondary status of each, in the medium that makes the most sense.

Marketing Goal: Making the List

When birthdays and year-end holidays approach, parents of younger children (says ages three and under) will make "the parents' list" of the toys they might buy, including those they will influence others to buy for their child. This list is based upon what each parent believes their child's preferences to be as well as their own desires. Parents of older children (age about four plus) often ask their children to compose "the kids' list" that they rely heavily upon. Typically, it's a listing of ten or fewer items the child wants. Parents will often ask children to prioritize the list so that they know which toys the children want most. In fact, for every toy a given child puts on the list, there are literally thousands of toys that do not make it. Having your toy placed on the lists (the parents' list for younger kids and the child's list for older kids) is the most important goal for any marketing plan.

Blockbuster marketing helps great toys make the lists, thus helping them in their quest to become blockbuster toys. But I'll add a word of caution. Blockbuster marketing cannot help a weak or even mediocre toy achieve blockbuster status. Several studies I conducted demonstrated that throwing more advertising dollars—and great advertising—behind so-so toys did not significantly increase sales. But throwing more great advertising behind great toys launched them into the stratosphere. Blockbuster marketing must begin with a blockbuster toy that truly connects emotionally with children and parents in unique ways.

You will notice throughout these chapters that many of the toys discussed are the same ones used as examples in the past chapters. That's because blockbuster toys often have several elements working in concert that helped them achieve greatness.

CHAPTER 13

Blockbuster Public Relations

The role of public relations has changed over the years. In days past, this was limited to promoting the corporate viewpoint of a specific company action. It was oftentimes used as damage control when things went terribly wrong. This might have occurred if a product, toy, etc., harmed its user, if it was discovered that the company was paying laborers a less-than-living wage in a Third World country, or for dozens of other reasons. The public relations discipline was far more reactive than proactive.

Things have changed. Today, public relations plays a much broader role, generating awareness, excitement, and desire for a plaything even before formal advertising begins. It can create stellar events that get noticed by core consumer enthusiasts (opinion leaders), consumers at large, and the media (reporters) by using various tools such as news releases, media relations, community events, newsletters, promotions, and sponsorships. Such tools can help launch a toy and take it to blockbuster status even before one dollar has been spent on advertising.

Public relations efforts often depend on the media to then perpetuate the buzz by writing favorable articles about the plaything. Those in the media are often willing participants because they like to hunt for and report about the Next Big Thing, which in turn sells newspapers and keeps broadcast viewers engaged. The 2003 American International TOY FAIR was attended by 892 print and broadcast reporters, as well as 52 representatives from eleven countries, according to the Toy Industry Association. Public relations utopia happens when the full force of this media army takes over and, without the marketer spending one dime, spreads a story from newspaper to newspaper, from radio interview to radio interview, from television interview to television interview. Because the media is thought to be a credible source of information, the listening consumers (mostly parents) often pay closer attention than if it were paid advertising. In this way, the credible message spreads and parents become far more aware of a toy than they had been previously, making them more alert should their child request the toy.

Michele C. Litzky, president of Litzky Public Relations, which specializes in selling to kids and their parents, says:

> Creating a blockbuster in the toy industry is not an easy task. For one thing, kids are fickle. You can never truly predict what toys, games, books, or movies they are going to embrace as part of their day-to-day culture. And, there are a lot of companies with products competing for their discretionary income. It's easier when you rely on their parents. And that's where astute public relations come into play. Think Tickle Me Elmo. Once Rosie O'Donnell decided it was a "must-have" and the frenzy began, there wasn't a parent anywhere who didn't want their child (often months-old infants) to be part of the Elmo experience.

This is not completely a recent phenomenon. When a 1950 article in the *New Yorker* featured Silly Putty, sales rose beyond 250,000 units in just three days. That was one of the first indications of the power that the media can exert in the sale of a plaything, particularly when the media reaches the attention of adults. It instantly propelled Silly Putty from a mere novelty to a blockbuster toy.

Having mentioned the immense impact public relations can

have, it should be noted that the impact of any given public relations effort can be quite beyond a marketer's control. First, the toy must be "newsworthy." If the media thinks the toy is a yawn, they will not give it ink. Second, it requires that the media decides to write a positive story. Third, it requires that several media outlets jump on board so that the news story reaches a critical mass. Fourth, it depends upon whether the news is motivating enough to parents and/or their children. These are not easy to achieve, which is why each year only a couple of toys are hailed as "potential blockbusters" by the media. The media is highly critical, fickle, and not always in agreement. So while public relations efforts have tremendous potential to help launch a new toy, they are also the biggest wildcard in the marketer's deck.

In some blockbuster successes, the public relations efforts worked well beyond anyone's dreams because of the *X Factor,* meaning that the toy received an immense though unexpected boost. This is the case, for example, when a celebrity suddenly fawns over a new toy to the excitement of the listening public. Such occurrences are very rare and cannot be relied upon.

Though the results of public relations efforts can be rather unpredictable, the stories of playthings that were catapulted to blockbuster status due to such efforts can provide some insights. When done well, public relation efforts plant the seeds of a story about a toy that fulfills needs in a unique way. First and foremost, it must be newsworthy.

Teddy: Creating a Toy to Fit the Moment

For most of the history of the world, toys were never, ever newsworthy. They simply didn't matter all that much. They didn't create jobs, war, peace, famine, or abundance. They were *just* toys. But every now and then, they reached prominence in unexpected ways. One of the earliest, if not the earliest, demonstrations of this in the United States was the introduction of the Teddy Bear, as noted in an earlier chapter.

The bear was not only modeled after the one that Theodore Roosevelt supposedly "saved," but the president also endorsed the use of his name for the toy. That was one of the greatest moments in the history of toys and public relations. Of course, there were no public relations professionals at hand trying to entice the president do such a thing. The toymaker, Morris Michtom, simply sent his creation to the president and asked him if he could use his name. A delighted president said "yes."

Michtom's creation was *on emotional target* and *on trend*, but he also noted the newsworthiness of moment. The actions of the president to "save the bear" were reported everywhere, and so too did news of Teddy's Bear spread. Reporters reported. Parents bought. Children wanted to save it, hug it, and be its nurturer and protector. Michtom created a toy to fit a "newsworthy" moment. That could never have happened had this toymaker not been wearing his marketer's cap. The public relations that sprang from the event were fun and playful, and so was the toy.

Teddy Roosevelt wasn't the last president to be associated with a toy. It was reported that President Kennedy played publicly with a yo-yo. An astronaut even brought one aboard the space shuttle *Atlantis*. These moments made the news and they undoubtedly helped the yo-yo keep its prominence. But these and other examples were the exceptions and not the rule in those days. Toys, by and large, remained *just* toys for a very long time, unworthy of being newsworthy. But that was about to change.

Cabbage: Steady Build

Cabbage Patch Kids came to international prominence in 1983 when the demand for the toys suddenly outstripped supply. News reports appeared of parents unable to get their child a Cabbage Patch Kid. That sent more parents to camp outside of stores in hopes that they could be there when a new shipment of the elusive doll arrived. The increased demand depleted supplies further and a major shortage resulted. That created more news stories. It was estimated that by early 1984, over 3 million Cabbage Patch Kids dolls had been sold, and yet there were still children who had asked but not received their doll. That made it a newsworthy, human-interest story. The manufacturer ramped up production to meet the demand. At the height of the craze, according to one source, Cabbage Patch Kids reached annual sales of over $600 million.

Unlike the development of the Teddy Bear, which was a toy made to capture the moment, the lesson that comes from the success of Cabbage Patch Kids is quite different. Contrary to the popular notion that they were an overnight success, Cabbage Patch Kids had been around since the late seventies (first known as Little People). The dolls were beautifully crafted and had a unique, emotionally laden concept (adoption). The toymaker used public relations quite well, steadily gaining consumer interest through press conferences, special events, news releases, and talk-show appearances. The steady build set the stage for a possible blockbuster breakout. Once the shortage occurred, the national media helped the toy achieve the blockbuster status it deserved. Public relations, at its best, simply puts great toys in the right situations that have high potential to be newsworthy, and then it sits back and lets fate take control. That's the Cabbage Patch Kids story.

After that moment, toys acquired "routine" prominence with the news media as never before, and the media began to take greater interest in the new toys that are exhibited at the annual TOY FAIR. They began to write more articles about which toys may be "hot" at Christmas, as well as which toys may be in short supply. The *Los Angeles Times,* for instance, ran a story in its February 10, 2003, issue about the then upcoming 2003 American International TOY FAIR. It stated that "among the candidates for the 'next big thing' are Barbie of Swan Lake, a poster-thin telephone to hang on the wall and a battery-operated dog." In its February 24 issue, *BusinessWeek* ran a story entitled, "What's Making Toyland Buzz," in which they, too, featured several toys that caught the attention of the reporter. That kind of exposure fuels the public's awareness of and appetite for the new toys. The media is also quick to report when no Next Big Thing is present. The same *Los Angeles Times* story cited above mentioned that 2002 was lackluster for the toy industry, which "failed to produce a marquee toy like the Cabbage Patch Kids or Furby to ignite the market." The media, then, is always on the hunt for the Next Big Thing. Cabbage Patch Kids created that shift.

Tickle: The Full Plan and the X Factor

Tickle Me Elmo, 1996.
Courtesy of Fisher-Price.

The Tickle Me Elmo doll debuted at the American International TOY FAIR in February of 1996. It was a great toy, following the path of most great toys that year: gaining distribution for the holiday season, readying its advertising efforts, and having some notable press. But even great toys sometimes need serendipitous moments to become blockbusters. That moment came on October 2 of 1996, when Tickle Me Elmo was featured as a prize on the "Rosie O'Donnell Show." The world was suddenly abuzz. A mere thirteen days later, on October 15, *USA Today* proclaimed that Tickle Me Elmo was one of the hottest toys. Several weeks after that, Bryant Gumbel played with the toy on "The Today Show." The day after Thanksgiving, retailers were sold out.

One consumer who lived through the episode posted a three-page summary of his experience on the Internet. Through his words, the power of the full marketing plan can be detected. He stated that he was watching the Macy's Thanksgiving Day Parade on television, noting the "Sesame

Street" float go by, which included Big Bird and Elmo. Soon thereafter, a Tickle Me Elmo commercial appeared in the break. He decided he had to get one. But with the groundwork laid by earlier public relations efforts, culminating in endorsements from national celebrities such as Rosie O'Donnell (*X Factor*), there were none to be had. News reports spread of parents waiting for shipments to arrive. That motivated more parents to seek out this elusive toy (which was on the shelf for many months, in ample supply, prior to the craziness). TYCO, the manufacturer, shipped in more units, but not all of them would arrive in time for Christmas. More pandemonium ensued. The price of Tickle Me Elmo was bid up as people began to buy them from consumers who bought earlier (whoever thought toy scalpers would ever invade the industry?). One report declared that a Tickle Me Elmo with a list price of $30 went for $750. Caught off guard, the manufacturer immediately ramped up production. By Christmas of 1996, over 1 million Tickle Me Elmo dolls had been shipped, making it a blockbuster toy.

The Tickle Me Elmo story shows the importance of an integrated program (e.g., float in a prominent parade, advertising, and early public relations efforts). The communications program was there, ready for the magic of the *X Factor* to happen. Here's how one executive puts it all into perspective. Craig Spitzer, now vice-president of marketing research for Fisher-Price, who was an executive at TYCO at the time of the Tickle Me Elmo explosion, says:

> What propels a toy to greatness depends on how you want to define greatness. There is the greatness of a "beyond-all-expectation, sold-out-before-Christmas toy." This is often the result of a lucky confluence of events. In the case of Tickle Me Elmo, the design of the toy was very good. It had a popular but at that time undermarketed character in Elmo. It featured contagious laughter. It was wondrous to see and try on the shelf at retail. Our PR efforts ensured samples reached the media outlets as

they should, but who knew that Bryant Gumbel would fall in love with Elmo and hold and play with him for the better part of an hour on "The Today Show"? Who knew how much Rosie O'Donnell would love the toy and work it into her show? Who knew how good Jay Leno's first pass at a joke about it would do, or that he and David Letterman would start joking about it nightly? It starts with a good toy, but when everything else falls into place, it's like riding a bicycle downhill with no brakes. You just hope you can steer yourself to safety while you are enjoying the ride. There is another kind of toy greatness as well. That is when a toy is such a great fit with children that it lasts for decades. The Fisher-Price Rock-a-Stack is one of these. It does not get simpler. It has colorful rings of descending size, which you stack onto a post with a rocking base. For the eight-month-old child of 2003, stacking those rings, rocking the stack, then dumping and teething on them is as much fun as it was for the children of 1993, 1983, and earlier. This is a great toy because it is a great fit with both what children are capable of doing and with what engages them.

The Psychology of Hype and Shortage: A Caution

Why do consumers (all of us) buy the media hype, whether intended by the manufacturer or not? Here's my guess. Children want a toy that they find emotionally satisfying. The media often highlights that aspect of the toy and helps spread the word to parents. Parents want to be sure that they give their child a plaything they desire. That's why parents are willing to suffer long lines that the media sometimes helps to create. During the holiday season of 1998, I was in a line waiting to buy a Furby at a toy store. I was surprised to discover that some of the parents waiting in the line did not know what a Furby was, nor had their children actually asked for it. They were there solely to get a toy that other parents wanted, and they were afraid that someday before the holiday their child *might* ask for it. For these parents, it was a *"just in case"* purchase. Because consumers have now experienced toy shortages, they are more alert to media accounts that shortages exist. Because such shortages are now deemed "newsworthy," reporters don't want to miss the scoop of the year.

That's my take on the basic psychology of the craziness that's been going on since 1983. We have seen it with other notable blockbusters such as Tamagotchi (virtual pet) and Pokemon (Pocket Monsters), and we are beginning to see it in Yu-Gi-Oh! During its first three years in Japan, the franchise sold 7 million video games and 3 billion cards, which are used to pit fanciful, powerful creatures against each other. The WB television series is about a shy high-school student named Yugi who gets sucked into a realm of monsters and battles. Because of its popularity, the media is on the now routine lookout for shortages. A prominent newspaper declared in 2002 that the toys that have sprung from this entertainment property in the U.S. are in short supply. "Some retailers foresee shortages," it declared. It quoted one retailer as saying, "If we get a shipment on a Wednesday, I'm sold out by Friday." That media coverage will undoubtedly fan the flames of interest and create an even deeper shortage.

Personally, while I appreciate the role that solid and thoughtful public relations can play in selling most toys, I'm not in favor of the ultrahyped approach, often fueled by the media. Ultrahyped toys are at risk of burning out faster because they have a frenzied cycle: interest—shortage—hype—more shortage—more hype—frantic purchase—demise. The purchase becomes a goal in itself (over and above the satisfaction the toy can bring). Once the purchase is fulfilled, the toy is in danger of being crossed off of the parent's and child's list forever (been there, done that). The toy used up the emotional energy that parents and children spent to obtain it. If the "news" in year two is more about shortage (or elimination of the shortage) and less about how the toy is better than last year, then the toy is in trouble.

The truth is, most toys in short supply were not projected to be blockbusters, nor did their manufacturers intentionally create the shortage. The manufacturers were as surprised as anyone that the marketing campaign (often led by public relations efforts) suddenly caught on fire. In most cases, manufacturers are simply conservative with production orders because they don't want to overproduce, which is very risky in the toy business. They prefer to produce just a little bit more than they believe is needed, ensuring that they have just enough toys for the children who want them. Since only a couple of toys reach blockbuster status each year and become in short supply because of it, it's simply not prudent to keep *all* toys in short supply in hopes the shortage will make the news. The lost revenues would be staggering.

When a toy becomes a sudden blockbuster, the manufacturer has to scramble to meet orders. That's the first time it suddenly realizes it has a blockbuster on its hands. The problem it then faces is how to manage a blockbuster. Not wanting to risk losing sales, a manufacturer might mistakenly overproduce to meet what it believes to be ongoing demand. If demand suddenly falls from the dizzying heights, it can leave the manufacturer with heavy debts and bankruptcy. Coleco, the manufacturer of Cabbage Patch Kids dolls during the height of the dolls' popularity, filed for Chapter Eleven bankruptcy a couple of years after the dolls' sudden rise to blockbuster status. Mattel's blockbuster Intellivision not only bottomed out with the video-game category a couple of years after its rise to blockbuster status, but it was responsible for the near-death experience of giant Mattel itself. Manufacturers have very long memories, and the prospect of overproducing is a recurring nightmare. It's quite understandable, then, that subsequent video-game introductions were cautiously produced, such as Nintendo 64 (1996) and PlayStation 2 (2000), both of which had initial demand outstrip supply.

Some marketers recommend keeping the interest of a blockbuster alive by maintaining the shortage. In their book

The Fall of Advertising and the Rise of PR, Ries and Ries state, "At the first sign of a potential fad, you put on the brakes. Reduce production, reduce distribution points, and be unavailable to the media. You want to stretch out the adoption rate and turn the fad into a trend." That might account for the tactics used by Ty in marketing Beanie Babies. As mentioned in an earlier chapter, Ty employed the unique strategy of "retiring" Beanie Babies in order to prolong interest and demand, while fueling a collector's market. And it worked for quite a time, the craze hitting its pinnacle around 1997. It certainly gave greater longevity to Beanie Babies than would have been achieved had Ty mistakenly overproduced the line.

But trying to sustain a shortage for its hype value can be as dangerous as overproducing. Kids and parents might turn to alternatives. Loyal consumers can become disgruntled. The trade can become irate over sales they are missing. And as said previously, the emotional capital expended by consumers can get used up quickly.

The Best Kind of Public Relations

The best kind of public relations does not worry about creating rumors of shortages, real or contrived. That's a fool's trap (and ethically dubious). The best PR efforts focus on the benefits of the toy and the smiles it can bring. The best kind of public relations plods along slowly, not with sudden hype but with solid purpose and determination, knowing full well that the toy has the right ingredients to achieve blockbuster status. The Cabbage Patch Kids brand, as noted earlier, is an example of this.

Another one of the best examples of an ongoing public relations campaign is that of PEZ Candy. The manufacturer, in fact, claims to not advertise at all. It relies on routine mentions in newspapers and television shows, media coverage of collectors, and, of course, good presence in stores. It stays current by changing the dispensers' heads to reflect trends, fads, characters, and holidays, which becomes newsworthy. It's probably the best example of a toy/candy brand that was never overhyped, yet relied upon favorable and routine public relations to create an ongoing presence. It has lasted decades.

The Barbie doll decided to run for the presidency in 2000, and the story was covered again and again. One news report stated, "With the battle for nominations seemingly over, candidates in the 2000 presidential election suddenly face an unexpected rival, one who threatens to capture much of the younger electorate . . . Barbie for president. . . . The candidate will attend both Republican and Democratic conventions. . . . Barbie's beliefs closely parallel those of Vice President Al Gore, giving him another competitor. . . . Mattel will set up voting booths in Toys R Us stores in major cities across the United States . . . allowing children to vote for their candidate." Mattel created an official campaign Web site to convey Barbie's beliefs, to allow girls to vote on issues close to their hearts, and to teach girls about the presidential election process. In a press release at the time of the launch, Anne Parducci, senior vice-president of Mattel at the time, stated, "Barbie doll's run for Presidency embodies all that she strives to teach girls—aim high, work hard and stand up for what you believe in. We are proud to be a partner in the continuing efforts to educate girls about the potential they hold, and encourage them to follow all of their dreams."

The news that Mattel created and fostered was not about a toy shortage, not about parents waiting in lines, and certainly not about a company that was trying to diminish supply. It didn't depend upon the chance endorsement of a celebrity. It was solely about the toy, its reinvention in a way that was unique and compelling, and its relevance to significant contemporary events. It got children involved. It offered qualities that parents could not only accept but embrace. It had national and even international scope, which fostered media attention. It was also inspired, playful marketing, because *it engaged everybody to join in the fun:* kids, parents, adults, politicians, and writers. You can just imagine the first time that toy designer offered the idea to the Mattel management, and the excitement that must have darted around the table as ideas were immediately generated for great public relations.

Great public relations do one more thing. They help convey the emotional needs the toy can satisfy and plant the seeds for how the child might be transformed as a result. Michele C. Litzky, president of Litzky Public Relations, comments:

> I was part of the team that brought e-kara Real Karaoke to the United States from Japan, where it was huge. The premise behind the product was that with e-kara, the first portable and affordable handheld karaoke system, *everyone* could live out their pop-star fantasies. We all had visions of little girls (and not-so-little girls) everywhere, standing in front of the mirror—hairbrush in hand—pretending to be Britney Spears or Destiny's Child. Well, e-kara brought the fantasy to life. Our job was to bring the fantasy to tweens and teens, which we achieved through onstage, live-audience product demos in both New York and Los Angeles. These "casting calls" gave thousands of people the chance to experience e-kara and two lucky girls the opportunity to "star" in the first e-kara TV spot. To reinforce this initiative and to introduce e-kara to the millions of other girls and their parents who didn't get to the casting calls, we made sure that e-kara was front and center in every medium they came across—newspapers, magazines, radio station give-aways, product placement on TV. E-kara Real Karaoke was named the number-one girls' toy of 2001.

A president of the United States protected a bear, and children could too with the Teddy Bear. Parents in the real world adopt children, and girls can be transformed into parents by adopting Cabbage Patch Kids. Someday a woman will be elected president of the United States, but today any girl can be transformed into president when playing with Barbie. That's the story, and great public relations help bring the transformation process to life.

The Next Big Thing: Basic Principles

• For toys currently under development, the toymaker's challenge is to think ahead about how the toy might utilize public relations. Is the toy highly "newsworthy" to begin with? If it is not, you must rethink the basic benefits and features of the toy itself, for if it is not newsworthy, one must wonder if it is unique and compelling enough to gain the attention of children or parents, let alone the media.

• But don't be newsworthy for the sake of generating news. The toy, first and foremost, must fulfill children's and/or parents' emotional needs.

• Invent toys that come out of the moment (e.g., Teddy Bear).

• Use public relations that are step by step, solid, and sure (e.g., Cabbage Patch Kids).

• The public relations plan should be fun, playful, and sprinkled around (e.g., Tickle Me Elmo). It should be engaging, help convey the emotional needs that the toy satisfies, and even help consumers see how the child might be transformed in fantasy or reality as a result of owning the toy (e.g., Barbie for President).

• While a manufacturer will seldom have to manage a "sudden" blockbuster, it should have a plan in place in case a toy does break through to such status. How will it manage production? How will it prevent the toy from sizzling too fast and crashing too early?

• Playing with "shortage" is dangerous. While PR efforts to create a sense of scarcity might increase interest, they can just as likely create situations out of the marketer's control. There's also another relevant viewpoint (that I share): Every child who honors the toy by requesting it, and every parent who honors the toy by taking the time to search for it, should be able to get it. After all, a toymaker makes smiles . . . not shortages.

CHAPTER 14

Blockbuster Advertising

While public relations efforts can help a toy in its march toward blockbuster status, their effect is often too unpredictable to rely upon. Advertising, then, becomes of prime importance to the manufacturer because they can control it.

I have worked on hundreds of toy commercials over the years, and I can attest that great toys tend to lead to great advertising and mediocre toys tend to lead to mediocre advertising. It is true that blockbuster toys on occasion get shackled with mediocre advertising and are hurt by it. But it is very rare (never in my experience) that great advertising can sell a mediocre toy. That's because kids and parents want to know about the toy, what it does, and what it can do for them. So the toy must be the star of the advertising, often living or dying on its own merits. In that context, advertising's role is simply to bring the blockbuster toy to life, thus illuminating the emotional need it satisfies, and oftentimes highlighting the very way in which the child can be transformed (in reality or fantasy) as a result of owning the blockbuster toy.

In my first book, *Creating Ever-Cool,* I commented that "effective" advertising seems to be a subjective evaluation. I still agree with that. A piece of advertising can help support sales of a whopping $200 million worth of product, but if the goal was to sell $300 million, the advertising may well be judged a failure. Alternatively, advertising can help sell $300 million worth of toys and beat the sales goal, but if management hates the advertising, it can also be deemed ineffective. I've seen both situations, and many more. The subjective nature of the evaluation is compounded by the fact that the success of the advertising is closely linked with the blockbuster potential of the toy, as discussed earlier.

Despite such subjectivity, the following guidelines can be used to develop great advertising. These guidelines build upon principles I outlined in *Creating Ever-Cool*.

Creating Toys that Lend Themselves to Advertising

Toymakers need to think about how their toy will be ultimately advertised, even as the toy is under development. They need to build in features, play patterns, and emotional benefits that lend themselves to advertising. If the toy's features or benefits are too subtle or difficult to demonstrate in advertising, the ability of the advertising to communicate the toy's uniqueness will be diminished. Some features such as fragrance or complex character personalities, for example, can be very difficult to demonstrate in advertising. This can hamper the toy's ability to communicate its blockbuster qualities. So toymakers must realize that how they build the toy today will impact the success of the advertising tomorrow. The more overtly playful the toy, the more playful the advertising will be. The toy qualities that tend to make for great advertising are these.

• Toys with highly visual, easily demonstrable, unique features.

• Toys with demonstrable play patterns that a child can easily be shown duplicating.

• Toys with simple, yet highly emotional benefits that a child and/or adults can readily express in the advertising.

Once the right toy is built with the right features to lend itself to advertising, the advertising process begins.

Synergy Model

Effective advertising has a single-minded, strategic synergy. That is, the key elements embodied in the advertising work seamlessly together to communicate a focused, relevant, brand-differentiated message about the toy. This strategic synergy is depicted in the Synergy Model in exhibit 4. The Synergy Model begins at the top and moves clockwise, starting with communicating the toy's blockbuster, unique product feature(s), which propel the play pattern. These need to support the brand's emotional benefit, which is expressed in a blockbuster (meaningful) toy name, which is brought to life in a blockbuster advertising approach. When the linkage among these components is strong, advertising is more likely to be effective. When the linkage is weak, advertising is more likely to be ineffective.

Hence, advertising effectiveness is highly related to marketing decisions that began long before the first advertising concept was presented, such as the toy's features, play pattern (and inherent emotional benefit), and the selection of an appropriate name. Advertising, after all, serves up the entire brand package.

Let's review the model in more detail, using a commercial for Olympic Gymnast Barbie that aired in the 1990s.

• Beginning: The commercial opens as an animated Olympic Gymnast Barbie (computer-generated graphics) carries an American flag, runs up the steps to the stadium and past the Olympic flame, and stands in front of the cheering crowd.

• Middle: Cut to real girls who are playing with Olympic Gymnast Barbie, having her do cartwheels and somersaults with the aid of a "tumbling ring" that Barbie can rotate around.

• End: Barbie wins the gold with the help of the girls. The real girls high-five each other as they feel the thrill of the win,

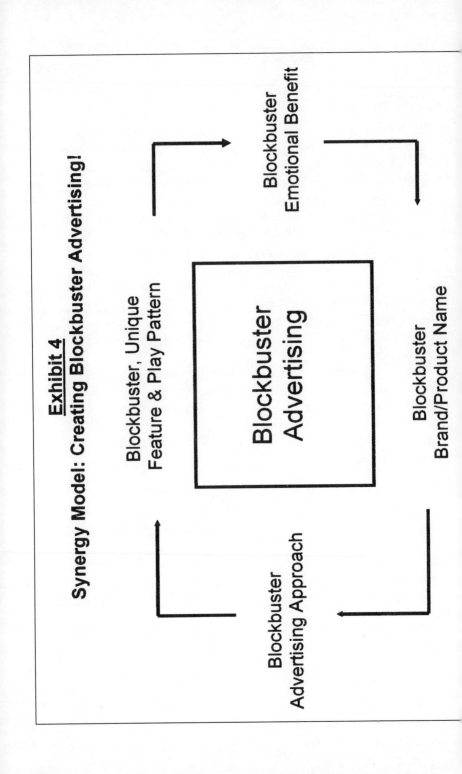

Exhibit 4

Synergy Model: Creating Blockbuster Advertising!

Blockbuster, Unique Feature & Play Pattern

Blockbuster Emotional Benefit

Blockbuster Advertising

Blockbuster Brand/Product Name

Blockbuster Advertising Approach

and then an excited animated Barbie is shown with her medal, an American flag behind her.

Advertising effectiveness begins with identifying the brand's single most relevant and unique product feature(s), as expressed by the child. In this case, the Barbie doll is a gymnast and has agility aided by a "tumbling ring" feature that allows her to do cartwheels and somersaults. The key feature leads to a great play pattern (in this case, competition and "Olympic" play). The emotional benefit is the aspiration to win a gold medal. Hence, the Olympic play pattern allows the child to imagine what it would be like to "transform" into a real gold medalist. The brand name supports the play pattern. Finally, the key feature(s), play pattern, associated emotional benefit, and brand name are brought to life through the advertising. For Olympic Gymnast Barbie doll, the commercial featured only those items and activities central to being an Olympic gymnast, such as the Barbie doll's ability to spin and perform gymnast moves, her outfit, and, most importantly, the emotional payoff as she wins the gold medal! Finally, computer-generated imaging brought the Barbie doll's persona to life. In this seamless effort, a focused point of view emerges that communicates what the brand has to offer: key product feature(s), play pattern, associated emotional benefit, reinforced by a brand name, and brought to life with the advertising. The more often these elements work together, the greater the likelihood that the child will be able to understand the toy's advantages.

If any of these elements is weak, the whole message will be weakened. If the toy does not have a product feature that kids like over and above competitive offerings, the advertising will suffer. If the feature does not lead to a compelling play pattern or emotional benefit, the advertising will suffer. If the toy's name has no linkage back to either a feature, play pattern, or emotional benefit, or if it is hard to remember or too cumbersome to say, the advertising will suffer. If the advertising is unfocused, attempts to communicate too many features unrelated to the core play pattern or emotional benefit, or uses elements that interfere with as opposed to reinforce the main message, it will suffer. And in the confusion, kids will deem the advertising, and the toy it conveys, as not for them, and the toy will never make "the list."

While the above example used a commercial directed to the child, the same applies to parent-directed advertising. The difference, of course, is that the latter needs to provide parents with the relevant benefits the child will derive from the plaything, as discussed in chapter 2 (e.g., will the child be happier, more developed, more successful, more imaginative, etc., as a result of using the toy?).

Advertising Execution

The advertising, as stated, brings the core essence of the toy to life. More often than not, it will do so in a thirty-second television commercial, since that remains the primary means of reaching kids and frequently parents (though print is often used for parents as well). There are many ways to *execute* the advertising. David Ogilvy, founder of Ogilvy & Mather Advertising, would search for what he called the *big idea*, referring to an approach that would grab attention and communicate the brand's benefit in an intriguing, unique way. There are many places to look for that big idea in a kid's world, and the following is a partial list. Each is a possible way of communicating the toy to gain the attention of children or their parents. In my experience, we tend not to explore enough of these approaches, and we settle too early. These avenues should be addressed in any exploratory.

Blockbuster Demonstrations: This approach uses a dramatic demonstration of the toy's benefit. Past advertising for Slinky simply lets the toy demonstrate what it does. Hula Hoop advertising displays children mastering the art of the Hula Hoop.

Blockbuster Problem/Solutions: This approach shows the problem, and then reveals the solution provided by the toy.

Cabbage Patch Kids needed to be adopted by a parent. In the introductory advertising in the early eighties, a child "adopted" a Cabbage Patch Kid, in the presence of her real family, by promising to be a good parent. That helped any child viewing at home to imagine that they, too, could transform into an adoptive parent by giving the Cabbage Patch Kids a home.

Characters: Real or imagined characters might also endorse the toy. Various characters are used successfully for selling preschool toys to parents who trust the characters to both make the child happy and to motivate them to learn.

Testimonials: This approach uses loyal, real-life consumers to endorse the toy. Advertising in the preschool arena has successfully used experienced mothers to endorse toys.

Spokespersons: In certain situations, experts or celebrities can be used to endorse toys. Educators and celebrities have been used to promote educational toys to parents. Care has to be taken, however, not to violate industry guidelines relating to the use of spokespersons when advertising to children. "Celebrities and real-life authority figures," state CARU guidelines (Children's Advertising Review Unit, which was established to promote responsible children's advertising), "may be used as product endorsers, presenters or testifiers. However, extra care should be taken to avoid creating any false impression that the use of the product enhanced the celebrity's performance."

Fantasy Worlds: Fantasy worlds or settings can bring a toy's benefits to life. Advertising for the Battleship Naval Combat Game has depicted admirals engaged in fanciful battle. The child can imagine and pretend what it would be like to be an admiral, too.

Cultural World: In this approach, the advertising makes use of popular (i.e., *cool*) music, language, sports, or relevant mood/attitude/action to associate the toy with a kid's life. But to do it well, *cool* must be born out of the toy, not just slapped onto it.

Care must be taken, in using all the above, to not mislead children or parents regarding the toy's performance or their own performance if they owned the toy, or to not exploit a child's ability to distinguish reality from fantasy. Children are a special audience to be protected. These and other issues will be discussed in a subsequent chapter.

Elements of Execution

Creating toy advertising is subject to debate on many particulars. Here are some of the recurring issues regarding advertising to children.

Toy Focus vs. Elements of Execution: In an attempt to gain a child's attention, advertisers use a huge array of devices such as music, computer graphics, animation, fantasy settings, characters, unusual camera angles and techniques, etc. Arguments arise as to whether the toy itself is being given enough attention, as opposed to the attention-getting techniques that are thought to be *cool.* In general, all techniques should be used to showcase the toy and help bring to life its key feature, play pattern, and emotional benefit. If the techniques do not do this, they are wasted.

Simplicity vs. Complexity: Some executives say advertisements have to be as simple as possible so that the youngest child within the target age group can understand them. This requires simple language and forms of humor. Others say this makes advertising lose the older children, who will deem this approach juvenile and then deem the toy too childish. Older kids want faster-paced, cooler, more complex images, they say, as well as more adultlike humor such as satire. In many cases, I have found that the best approach is to include communications that are simple to understand but served up with an older, cooler attitude, thus giving the younger children something to aspire toward without alienating older kids. In the entertainment world, the physical humor of Bugs Bunny entices younger viewers while his wit entices older ones.

Advertising should strive to achieve that same balance. This is harder, but worth trying to achieve.

Words vs. Music and Song: Some executives prefer music and sung copy to create a *cool* attitude. Other says it is in the interest of clear communication to have all key copy spoken plainly rather than sung. The answer to this debate is . . . it depends. Music and singing can add much to attitude development, particularly if the song is so enticing that children begin to sing it over and over. Many of us can still sing the words to the Slinky song from its early advertising. Still, if the lyrics are hard to understand, or if they are asked to bear the burden of communicating a complex piece of copy, then they are best spoken plainly. In fact, a combination of sung and spoken copy can be quite successful.

Boy vs. Girl Casting: When children are ages five to nine (where most of the traditional toys are sold), the separation of genders in terms of key desires, attitudes, and interests is strong. So during those years, most toys and advertising are split by gender. Girls are placed in commercials for girl-related toys and boys are placed in commercials for boy-related toys. The few toys and games that target both sexes during these ages are often more effective when they emphasize boys in the advertising and not girls. That's because some boys are still turned off by the presence of girls (though this is changing), whereas girls are not often turned off by the presence of boys. But this is a generality and there are plenty of examples to the contrary.

Here are a few more thoughts, and a reminder or two, to keep in mind when developing advertising for blockbuster toys:

- *For Kids:* Make the advertising amazingly playful. Give it energy, though this depends upon the nature of the toy. Make it something kids will talk about on the playground. Show the kids in the commercial having fun *in relation to,* and *because of,* the toy. Show children how they will transform in fantasy or reality (but always honestly).

• *For Parents:* Make the advertising inspiring. Make it warm, though this depends upon the nature of the toy. Make it something parents would be intrigued enough to talk with other parents about. Show the child enjoying the toy, being inspired by it, and, if appropriate, being transformed as a result of it.

• *For Kids and Parents:* Make the toy the focus of attention by showing the role it can play in their lives. Never talk down to kids or parents. Include a "magic moment" if it applies. That's the surprise moment in a commercial when the key exciting feature is suddenly revealed. Be honest; never promise anything that the toy can't deliver.

Paul Kurnit, president and founder of KidShop and an expert in kids and toys, provides these five simple principles for creating great toy advertising. They provide a nice summary.

1. Make a Great Product—one that is rich in relevant play and a complete play experience

2. Capture the Play Fantasy—create advertising that captures the fantasy of the play experience

3. Make the Product a Hero—use creative approaches and techniques that bring out the fun of the product, not the drama of the commercial

4. Distinguish the Product from the Competition—show why your product is the one to get

5. Create Badge Value—demonstrate why the product is a complement to a kid's lifestyle

The Next Big Thing: Basic Principles

• The toymaker's challenge is to think ahead on how the toy might be advertised, even as the toy is under development. Does the toy lend itself to advertising? Are the features, play patterns, and emotional benefits highly visual, demonstrable, and playful? Are there too many features without clear purpose?

- Does the advertising, once under development, have strategic synergy? That is, are all the elements working together to support the toy's key feature, play pattern, and emotional benefit?
- Have you considered the many potential advertising approaches that exist, or did you settle too early?
- Is the advertising as blockbuster as the toy? Does it demonstrate to the child or parent how the child will be transformed as a result of owning the blockbuster toy?

CHAPTER 15

Blockbuster Sales Promotions

The introduction of many blockbuster toys has taken on event status. In part, it is because many toys are now tied into entertainment properties and are "launched" when the film is released. Advertising and public relations efforts for entertainment releases are expended in a very narrow window of time, which serves to gain a large amount of awareness and excitement quickly. Even toys that are not associated with entertainment properties have to compete with such and, as a result, must attempt to create a lot of excitement around their offerings. They do it with advertising and public relations as we have discussed, and they also turn to sales promotions.

Assuming that your public relations program has achieved some buzz for your new toy, and your advertising has helped add to the excitement by moving a child (or parent) a bit closer to adding your toy to the all-important list, consumer sales promotions can help your toy be that much closer. Sales promotion tools include a spectrum of techniques including cross promotions, events and tours, sponsorships, sweepstakes and contests, premiums, in-movie placement, and various financial incentives such as coupons. These, in fact, may fall under the control of public relations and even advertising professionals. I decided to treat them separately because sales promotions, as a tool, have grown rapidly over the past decades as competition has intensified.

As with the other disciplines of advertising and public relations, it is important for toymakers to think through the potential promotion implications of the toy they are developing. The toys that lend themselves more easily to exciting sales promotion activities are those that will most likely get the attention of senior management as well as the consumer. The toymaker, then, must also wear a sales promotion hat.

KidScreen magazine routinely presents manufacturers with awards for the best youth promotions. Past nontoy winners have included such efforts as:

• The Rugrats Movie Post Cereal Ticket Giveaway, in which a cable station gave away tickets to the movie on millions of specially marked boxes of Post cereal brands.

• Tommy Hilfiger's Britney Spears Concert Tour Sponsorship, which included in-store retail promotions, sweepstakes, radio promotions, and store appearances by Britney Spears.

• The Find Godzilla and Win Promotion, in which consumers purchased fast-food meals and got clues to hunt for Godzilla (based upon a then upcoming feature film). The fact that the actual appearance of Godzilla was kept a secret helped create appeal for the promotion.

Says Tom Wong, senior vice-president of strategic insights and entertainment marketing at Strottman International, "There was a time when the job of sales promotions was to deliver short-term sales increases. Period. Now, as an integral part of the marketing mix, effective sales promotions are required to deliver sales while building brand image, awareness, and consumer loyalty." Tom lists three elements that make for great sales promotions:

• A relevant, emotional connection with the consumer—to get their attention and break through competitive clutter.

• The promise of a compelling consumer experience and value—to reward them for their time, trust, and money.

• The essence of the brand—the personality of the brand must be embraced, and its benefits delivered emotionally as well as in physical form.

"Add industry-changing innovation and you get the greatest sales promotions of all time," Tom concludes.

This is the world in which youth marketers now live. Though there are many types of sales promotions that toy manufacturers have used successfully, I will discuss just a few techniques in particular because of the attention and impact they typically garner. In a similar vein to public relations and advertising, the sales promotions efforts that work best tend to be those that help satisfy children's emotional needs (ways to have fun), often by helping them transform in some fashion that they hold dear (in fantasy or reality) and often in highly interactive ways. That is a hallmark of *playful marketing.*

The Blockbuster Event

Toymakers talk more and more these days about creating the BIG event. This uses any number of techniques that are designed to gain substantial awareness for the toy, generate excitement, and communicate its benefits. Video-game manufacturers, for example, have created a buzz around the release dates of new systems and software by specifying the time when a long-awaited toy will go on sale. Stores support the "launch," monitor the crowds, and deliver the new toy at the anointed hour (typically midnight) with considerable fanfare. While this technique helps create needed short-term excitement, it doesn't do much to help communicate the benefits of the toy or to create a deeper, longer relationship with the child or parent.

Promotional events that can have longer-term benefits are those that allow children to see, touch, and fully experience the broader view of the brand in ways that the toy, by itself, may not be able to accomplish. We already discussed the development of contests and championships in earlier chapters that did much to create excitement for specific toys (e.g., yo-yos, Frisbee, etc.) while connecting with core emotional needs such as mastery. Tours are another excellent example. For many years, those responsible for the Power Ranger franchise understood that children would delight in getting closer to the heroes they admire. This allows children to obtain a broader view of the brand by experiencing more of it. One such tour (i.e., Power Rangers Lost Galaxy Intergalactic Encounter Tour) took place at approximately fifty Wal-Mart stores across thirty-two markets. Kids got to explore a 5,000-square foot inflatable world of Power Rangers. In a previous tour, children were able to experience a space rocket simulator, thus pretending that they were spacemen. The flesh and blood Power Rangers were also on hand to meet and greet the children. This is a very special treat for those young ones who admire the Power Rangers' efforts to save the earth from alien invaders. These efforts allow children to experience the world of Power Rangers firsthand and, in so doing, help them feel more like Power Rangers themselves. They also help *transform* children, in fantasy, into the world of their heroes. Children, as you might expect, can also ask their parents for a Power Rangers toy and other merchandise at the nearby Wal-Mart. But the tour does more than create a quick sale. It helps children get closer to their dreams and fantasies in a highly interactive way, which is the essence of great, *playful marketing*. Tours expand and deepen the experiences children have with the franchise. When done well, these are fun outings for children and their parents, most of whom will be delighted by the happiness it brings to their children. At its best, this is what a great promotion idea can achieve.

To help celebrate the 100th birthday of the Crayola brand, Binney & Smith kicked off the Crayola ARTrageous Adventure, which entailed a cross-country bus tour in February 2003. It allowed children to "discover and interact with a new and unexpected world of Crayola products for the next century that includes out-of-this-box versions of their favorite art tools." Kids were able to color on the walls with Window FX markers, paint with melted crayons, and experience crayons that twist, click, and erase. As part of the festivities, children were also invited to name four new colors, thus empowering them to help create the next generation of products. The effort helped expand children's idea of what the Crayola brand is, while at the same time staying true to the brand's core benefit, that being to help children be transformed into creators. "We're bringing new twists on creativity to a new generation of children," said Stacy Gabrielle, a Crayola spokesperson. "We're celebrating a bright future ahead and recognizing where our first eight crayons have taken us since 1903."

Lego Systems sent six "Bionicle" vehicles across the country to places kids congregate, such as skate parks, arcades, and beaches. The vehicles were themed to each of the six Bionicle heroes. Kids got to play games, win prizes, and, most importantly, learn the mythology of Bionicle (back story of characters, etc.). It allowed children to see the broader view of the brand.

Events and tours that help immerse children in a bigger world of their toys can do a lot toward inspiring fun and involvement for the child, and blockbuster status for the toy. Toymakers need to ask themselves how their toys can use blockbuster events in ways that help children experience the toy in a broader way, while helping them transform into masters, creators, emulators, experience seekers, and such.

Blockbuster Premiums

Toys used as premiums for other products are commonplace today. As noted in an earlier chapter, the Cracker Jack brand was among the first foods, if not *the* first, to offer a prize in every box, thus helping it to achieve immense longevity and icon status for the brand and the toys. These were the first blockbuster premiums. Cereal companies now routinely insert prizes in their packages, often on a quarterly basis, in order to maintain interest. McDonald's followed with a similar concept in the quick-service restaurant category in order to sell its celebrated Happy Meal. The toys in the Happy Meal often tie into pop culture, so that McDonald's can connect with what interests today's kids and help their brand stay Ever-Cool.

Popular toys, when used well, can create opportunities for these other companies. This can also help good toys achieve blockbuster status, or help blockbuster toys retain their status. One example Tom Wong cites is that of McDonald's association with Hot Wheels. "The fact the kid's meal toys are commonplace today is a direct result of the strategic innovation embodied by McDonald's first Hot Wheels Happy Meal program," he says. "Hard as it is to believe, Hot Wheels was the first time a top toy product was given away with the purchase of a kid's meal. McDonald's and Mattel agreed that the stature and personality of these two megabrands were a perfect fit and that the free Hot Wheels toy would be as good as the retail product. The result: over twenty years later, Hot Wheels remains one of McDonald's most successful and enduring Happy Meal promotions."

The blend of a hot toy with a strong promotional partner also came together at the height of the Beanie Babies success, when McDonald's entered into an alliance with Ty to put Teenie Beanie Babies into Happy Meals. This is an amazing example of the potential that can be achieved when the right toy, at the right time, works in association with the right distributor and marketer. It was a great success story for both partners. The toys allowed children to be nurturers and collectors all at once. One estimate claimed that 80 million of the toys were distributed, increasing sales at some McDonald's stores by 30 percent over the previous year. The toy was sought by children, parents looking to fulfill children's requests, and adult collectors hoping that the items would increase in value over time.

Such success raises issues and this was no exception. Toymakers need to consider if such massive distribution is in the best long-term interests of the toy. Certainly, the short-term sales boosts are enormous. But the toymaker must remember that restaurants and food manufacturers are using the popularity of the toy premium to make the restaurant or food brand look contemporary and cool. These manufacturers will then switch to another, cooler premium when it presents itself. The toymaker has to be sure that such massive distribution does not hamper the long-term appeal of the toy.

Toymakers must ask themselves a couple of questions. What elements of my toy, or variation thereof, would work well in a kid's meal or cereal box without sacrificing the overall toy brand's long-term potential? How can these venues be used to deepen the child's experience with the toy, over and above the premium that is offered in the meal? Answers to these questions will not only safeguard the long-term potential of the toy but will often work in the interest of the manufacturer while providing children with greater, fun experiences.

The Blockbuster Movie Placement

Placing products in movies for the benefit of increasing interest in the item is relatively new to the marketing landscape, and so, many marketers still grapple with the strategy and objectives behind such efforts, as well as the mechanics of the timing, impact, and so forth. But when it works well, it can have an amazing impact. The early successful efforts that gained considerable notice were not directed at kids, per se, nor did they feature toys. Featured in the film *ET: The Extra-Terrestrial,* Reeses Pieces candy was used by the movie's central character, Elliott, to entice a hungry space alien out of his hiding spot. Elliott's attempt worked. It also worked for the brand, which reportedly had a sales increase of some 65 percent. The reason it worked was that the product was integral to the telling of the story. It wasn't just slapped into some scene (as many product-placement products are). It played a pivotal role. The same can be said for a product placed in the film *Men in Black,* starring Will Smith and Tommy Lee Jones. Ray-Ban Predator 2 sunglasses added the important finishing touch to the secret agents' attire. Sales of the sunglasses reportedly tripled to nearly $5 million after the release of the 1997 film.

In an interesting way, they helped adults connect with a harmless fantasy (being cool just like the *Men in Black*). The same might be said when James Bond speeds across the scene in a BMW roadster, which was also featured in recent films. By buying the car, we can feel that a little piece of the James Bond coolness rubs off on us.

Toy manufacturers have entered cautiously into this world. Care has been taken, as it should be, to be sure that the story is of central importance and that children are not subjected to an overly pressured "sales pitch" for a toy that is embedded in a movie.

One film that featured an array of wonderful childhood toys was, of course, *Toy Story*. In it, we saw the toys we grew up with and loved, like Mr. Potato Head and Army Men, as well as new ones like Woody and Buzz Lightyear. The *story* of *Toy Story* was superb, along with the heartfelt soundtrack by Randy Newman. That's what engaged adults and children, leading to demand for toys featured in the movie. In fact, you might be surprised to learn that the toys in *Toy Story* weren't "placed" there by toymakers hoping to sell more units. *Toy Story* was purely a creative idea sprung from an adult keenly in touch with the fascination and imagination of being a toy-loving kid. Ultimately, *Toy Story* generated demand for many toys, including "old" toys, because it brought them to life in such an appealing way that kids—and adults—fell in love with them.

The lesson, then, for any toymaker is not that you can slap a toy in a film and watch it be a success. The film must stand on its own as a delightful story. And if a toy has a central role in that story, it may benefit also. Only then can the joy brought by the film and the joy derived from the toy be realized in the joy it can provide the child.

Interestingly, video games have become "media venues" for other manufacturers' products. Mazda launched its new RX-8 not with an advertising campaign or by featuring it in a nearby showroom, but by including the vehicle in Sony's video game

Gran Turismo 3. In effect, the video game became the car's showroom two years before the metal debuted for real in Detroit. More and more, manufacturers will talk about placing products "in games" as much as they talk about placing them in movies. That demonstrates the power of the video-game platform. The toy, when imbued with story and a full sensory experience for the consumer, can become a much more robust marketing tool both for the toymaker and other manufacturers.

Blockbuster Synergy

As a toymaker, you will at times be on the periphery of a much larger promotional plan, playing one small role in someone else's design. This is often the case when you develop toys based upon an upcoming film. You not only must rely upon the success of the film, but also upon the synergistic success of the many promotional partners, because each will play a role in communicating not only excitement, but a shared point of view regarding the essence of the story and its characters. On the other hand, the toymaker may be at the center of the franchise, and must be responsible for orchestrating the efforts of studios, food companies, and others. Because of the multitude of companies involved, promotional synergy in bringing a property to life is vital.

One recent example was the introduction of the movie *Shrek*. DreamWorks lined up an array of promotional partners including Burger King with toys for its Kids Meal, Heinz Ketchup to cross-promote with its green variety, American Licorice Brand, which made a special variety for its Sour Punch candies, and Baskin-Robbins, which created new Shrek Flavors like Shrek Swirl. According to *KidScreen*, the integrated promotional strategy for *Shrek* connected with kids and parents across some 41,500 retail outlets. Each promotional partner benefited from the buzz created from the others, but each also helped to communicate appealing aspects of the film itself. The efforts allowed kids to have a broader Shrek experience in many interesting, unique, and *playful* ways that did not just reflect but also built upon the core idea of the franchise. That's what makes for great fun for kids, because it allows them to get closer to the story and the characters in ways that the film, by itself, would not be able to achieve. When developing sales promotions with a wide variety of partners, addressing this core challenge will help each partner—toymakers among them—create a synergistic plan that kids will truly enjoy.

A Final Promotional Note

There are many other types of promotional efforts that can also provide a deeper relationship between the brand and the child. Two, in particular, are worthy of note though they are not toy related. The first is the Oscar Mayer Talent Search. The promotion gives children the opportunity to perform the various brand jingles (e.g., "Wiener Jingle," "Bologna Song") in public in order to win prizes and money for their schools. It is fun, children get to try out their performance skills, and the winners are even featured in advertisements. In an interesting way, the promotion helps transform children into performers by giving all who compete their fifteen minutes of fame on stage. It connects with a strong emotional driver well beyond those associated with the food itself.

The second promotion worthy of note is Nickelodeon's The Big Help. The on-air promotion encourages children to pledge hours to help their communities in a variety of endeavors, from visiting the elderly to cleaning up beaches and parks. The motto is "share, clean, fix, visit, care, give, do." It helps transform children into responsible community helpers. It demonstrates the positive, larger role that a brand can play in the life of the child and the community. It's a very nice reminder that a promotion need not always be about a quick sale. It can also be about giving something special and enduring back to those children who are kind enough to ask for your products, and those parents who are kind enough to say "okay."

The Next Big Thing: Basic Principles

• The toymaker's challenge is to think ahead about how the toy, even while under development, might lend itself to playful sales promotions. But care has to be taken to ensure that short-term sales promotions do not threaten the long-term health and well being of the toy.

• Though there are many types of sales promotion tools, the best type help children experience a broader view of the toy specifically or the franchise in general. It helps children get closer to their fantasies and dreams, and therefore helps them transform into that fantasy or dream world.

• Sales promotions need not always be about "sales." They can also take a broader view of children's and parents' needs.

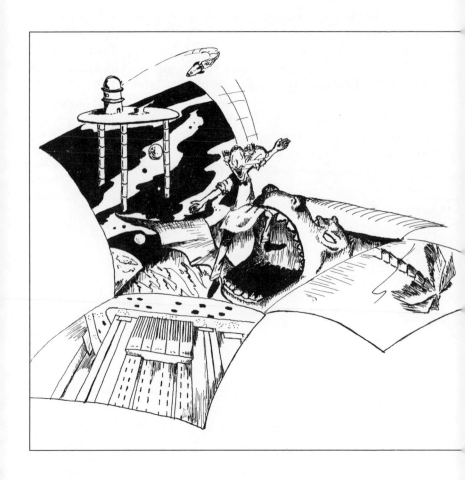

CHAPTER 16

Blockbuster Packaging

Let's assume you have tinkered long and hard and made a truly blockbuster toy, capable of transforming children and satisfying young hearts, thus generating millions of smiles on the faces of both children and their parents around the world. Let's assume you have launched a blockbuster public relations campaign for this new toy that helps create a notable buzz among the media, children, and their parents. Let's say you have created blockbuster advertising that clearly demonstrates the toy's key features, play patterns, and benefits. Let's also say that you have launched an exciting sales promotions effort that helps children and parents touch the larger aspects of the toy brand. With all that, your job is still not done.

As a toymaker, even one who works solely at a toymaker's bench, you still need to think about how you can use the toy's packaging in a way that will get noticed. How can it be block-buster in and of itself? This is very important because significant in-store dynamics occur that can raise a toy to great heights or banish it to oblivion. Children and parents often make a couple of visits to a toy store to cruise the aisles before a request or purchase is made. They are quick to pick up a package, examine it, turn it over to see what comes inside, and then move on to the next package to do the same. For children, this is often the last act they will perform before they decide which toy is "worth" requesting. Children want to be sure they get it right, for a toy that is placed on the long-honored list has a prominent place indeed, and children do not want to risk asking for a toy and then regretting it. Similarly, parents want to be sure they get it right. Because a child may have ten or so items on the list, and because Mom and Dad are not apt to get all ten, parents have a degree of latitude to select some items on the list over others. So parents will inspect the toy at the store to better understand its benefits, appropriateness, safety, and price. Some toys are also purchased by parents without a child's request, often because the parent wishes to surprise the child with something "out of the blue." So packaging, along with in-store displays, plays a key role. It has to be blockbuster in order to gain the attention of the child and the approval of the parent, and there are several ways to achieve that status.

Having dynamic and useful packaging and displays helps sell toys for the simple reason that it entices a strolling child or parent to momentarily pause and investigate. In the book *Why We Buy*, Paco Underhill states, "In a toy store, buyers spent over 17 minutes, compared to 10 for non buyers." Those who spent a longer time found something that grabbed their attention. That's what creating blockbuster packaging is all about.

The "No Package" Blockbusters

The best package is sometimes no package at all. If the toy is highly touchable, playable, and, many times, small, the best thing to do is let the child and parent actually touch and play with it. This leads to high interaction in the toy aisle (*playful marketing*). One of the best "no package" blockbusters was, and is, Beanie Babies. These small, plush, highly squeezable creatures are found in many configurations in the store: filling up bins, piled up in mounds, and stretched along counters. Because they have no package, they are placed virtually anywhere a child and a parent might encounter them, especially close to a cash register, which makes them a very good impulse purchase. Other blockbuster "no package" playthings have included small wind-up toys that scoot across a counter and, of course, balls of all types.

The basic purchase scenario for many no-packaged, low-priced toys is basically this: Child sees it, squeezes or activates it, Mom reaches out and does the same, a request follows, Mom considers the toy's appropriateness and price, a quick decision is often made, and, if favorable, the toy is immediately purchased. If the toy is of a higher price point, which requires more of Mom's consideration, or if she wants to surprise the child with the toy, she will say "no" or "maybe later," and then she'll make a final determination at a later date.

Some manufacturers and retailers have adopted the practice of assembling bigger items, such as play sets, to allow the child or parent to experience it. This was often a practice used by the Little Tikes Company. Founded in 1970, Little Tikes is a maker of innovative, high-quality, durable sandboxes, activity gyms, climbers, and many other toys. As floor display models, Little Tikes toys are climbed up, slid down, and ridden in store. The in-store display adds mightily to this plaything's blockbuster status because it allows children to experience the toy and the parents to view the child experiencing it. This can have dramatic impact on the children's and parents' interest in and involvement with the toy. Video-game developers know this all too well, which is why video-game stations have become commonplace; they allow the child and adult to try the new console or game even before the product arrives in the store. They also become "hubs" of word of mouth as various kids approach the station (often waiting in line to try a new game) and then discuss the product with others while playing.

One of the first examples of the power embedded in this "no package" approach began in 1943 when Richard James, a naval engineer, dropped a tension spring to the floor. Instead of just landing flat, the spring began to "walk" end over end across the floor. Realizing he had a toy, he brought it home, where his wife,

Betty, named it Slinky. It's interesting to note that during the Christmas of 1945, sales were slow. They did not reach block-buster heights until the Gimbels department store in Philadelphia decided that the toy needed to be demonstrated. Once the toy was out of the box, hundreds were sold in just a couple of minutes. What Slinky needed most of all was no pack-age at all. Later, a famous television commercial demonstrated Slinky, and millions of children wanted one for their own. For some toys, the blockbuster potential cannot be unleashed until they are seen, touched, probed, and/or activated. Playful inter-action is essential during the last-minute in-store experience.

Having no package then, either entirely or as part of display models, can be extremely powerful.

The "Touch Me" Blockbuster Package

A blockbuster component that swept through toy stores some years ago was the "touch me" package whereby the child or parent can reach through a hole in the package, give the toy a squeeze or push a button, and then watch as the toy per-forms its specialty. This is now commonplace in toy packaging, typically when there's an important feature or benefit. It allows the strolling child or parent the opportunity to experience the toy, while at the same time providing a package that can con-vey many other messages about product features and benefits. If the toymaker is lucky enough to get a parent's or child's fin-ger on the toy, he is that much closer to a request and a pur-chase, for the simple reason that the consumers will better understand what the toy does. One must wonder if Etch A Sketch, Jack in the Box, or any number of pull-string toys would have been as effective had they not allowed children to grab knobs, wind up springs, or pull strings. Yet as I pass a toy aisle even today, I'm amazed at the number of toys that have wonderful "touch me" possibilities but the packaging won't allow it, or features that could have supported the "touch me" quality were never built into the toy itself. And so, many toys on the shelves are passed by as children and parents reach for others that will allow them to play and interact. In a world in which children and parents face hundreds and even thousands of choices in each trip to the toy store, the odds favor those toys whose packaging allows them to be touched. As the toy is under development, then, the toymaker needs to ask the following question. Would my toy benefit from a "touch me" feature that would support both its key benefit and its package?

The "Useable" Blockbuster Package

A marble bag is a great example of a package that is highly useful. It allows the marbles to be easily transported by kids (and stored by parents). Children use the bag to take the precious marbles from room to room and from friend's house to friend's house, which facilitates play and social interaction. This same technique can be said to be in operation with Tinkertoy construction sets. The barrel-shaped, sturdy package conveniently stores all of the pieces (an aid to parents) and is easily transported by kids, enhancing play. This same basic, "useable" approach has been applied over the years to various brands, including LEGO building bricks and Crayola Crayons. Making the package useful can help great toys become blockbusters.

The "Toy as Package" Blockbusters

Some toys are, in fact, the package itself. We have already discussed a few of the most notable blockbusters, of which PEZ Candy is a great example. Here, the toy is the package for the candy. Over the years, the company has had minimal packaging in order to let the toy be prominent. The first PEZ dispensers did not have any packaging at all. They were sold with a couple of packs of candy and a paper insert, which were held to the PEZ dispenser with a rubber band. Over the years, PEZ has been packaged in other configurations, each of which allowed the toy to be well seen (e.g., cellophane overwrap, blister-packed cards, sealed poly bags, and shrink-formed overwrap).

The McDonald's Happy Meal has also been successful in using its package as the plaything. While the Happy Meal has playthings inside, the outside package often includes games and puzzles. In a very smart way, the play begins even before the child reaches into the bag.

Children's preschool books have greatly benefited from this approach. There has been nothing less than an explosion of toylike features and qualities built into the book itself, as mentioned in an earlier chapter. Push a button on the cover and you might hear bells ring or a character speak to coincide with the words or illustrations in the book. The book is toylike, and the toy is booklike. It has no package, per se, and yet the toylike quality of the book's cover creates interest and, in many ways, "houses" the words contained within.

Overall Design Elements

Toymakers must ask themselves if the package's design helps the toy stand out in a competitive set and if it clearly communicates key features, benefits, and exciting play patterns. In various research projects I have conducted on toy packaging over many years, it is always interesting to note just how fast the respondents can size up a toy based upon its package. At a mere glance, they might easily call one package "boring, plain, generic, not fun, and dated." The qualities of these packages are immediately transferred to the qualities they think the toy possesses. Another package might be deemed "fun, exciting, quality, and inspirational." The qualities of this package will also be transferred to the toy. Interestingly, these two toys may have nearly identical features. But one package allows the benefits of the toy to come to life, and the other does not.

And so there are many important design elements to keep in mind when developing blockbuster packaging. This applies to either a full package or any configuration of partial packages as discussed previously. The design elements that help a package compete are these:

• Does the package not just tell but demonstrate the toy's key features or benefits? Most children and parents first glance at the package's key visuals. If they are not enticing, the consumers won't take the time to read any of the copy. It's vital, then, that key visuals are used to demonstrate the features or benefits. Only when consumers *see* something that interests them will they actually pick up the box and read it.

• Does the package have a visual that associates it with the brand? Barbie packaging is often referred to as the Pink Wall. At a very quick glance, girls and moms know exactly what aisle is the Barbie aisle because of the color that has become synonymous with the brand.

• Does the package connect with other marketing elements? For example, scenes of the television commercial might be transferred to the packaging. That way, when children or parents see the packaging, their minds will recall the advertising and the benefits it conveyed.

• Does the package clearly convey the toy's name? You would be surprised how often packages do not. This can result in missed opportunities when a parent walks around the stacks of toys, trying to find the one their child asked for. You might think that parents, if confounded, will simply ask the salesperson for help, and that does happen. But remember that a parent often has a wish list that is far longer than the number of toys they will buy, so if a parent finds one toy in the store before another on the same list, that toy has the advantage. Clear name identification is an important factor.

• Does the package reflect the attitude or persona of the toy? Primary colors are often important for preschool toys because moms associate these colors with early childhood, and because such colors communicate a cheery, cute, youthful disposition. Primary colors are often a turnoff for children ages five and up because they associate those colors with "babies." Packaging intended primarily for older kids will need to be consistent with the older child's sensibilities: typically bolder designs and more action-oriented graphics (not cute or primary colors, which will "signal" that it's for younger kids).

- Does the package actually enhance play? Some packages become extensions of the toy and thus add to the play value. Dolls and action figures have come in packages that convert into play sets and environments. For example, the package might unfold to become a command center for an action figure or a cottage for a small doll.

- Does the package have the right elements to easily alert the parent to its contents and their safety and appropriateness? The latter is not just a matter of age grading but also general appropriateness. Video games, for example, are now labeled for levels of maturity. Toymakers need to alert parents to any issues they might object to.

Packaging should never be an afterthought. Just as advertising *is* the toy when viewed at home, packaging *is* the toy when viewed in the store. Toymakers should think about how the package might enhance and extend their toy concept. After all, no one knows their toy better than they do, or how to bring it to life better than they do. As such, just as toymakers need to understand and appreciate all of the other elements of marketing (public relations, advertising, and promotions), they also need to understand and appreciate packaging. For if the package is not as blockbuster as the toy itself, it will do a great disservice to the plaything.

Arvin Carlson, founder of Arvin Design, who has worked in packaging for such companies as Sega, Galoob Toys, and Mattel, offers these simple but powerful guidelines.

- The packages that communicate most effectively are the ones that are quick to read because they do a great job of focusing your product's message.

- Toy packages that tend to "put everything on every panel" end up with a cluttered message. Beware of this.

- Before starting any package development, visit several stores and check out your competition. Always review design alternatives in a real-world retail environment, with your package amongst the clutter and chaos of the competition. Establish the retail price-value of your package through its size, structure, unique color graphics, and communications, again comparing against the competition.

- Always remember, the package is your last chance to sell.

The Next Big Thing: Basic Principles

- The toymaker's challenge is to think about the package as an important extension of the toy itself.
- Does your package truly help convey the toy's key features, play patterns, and benefits?
- Does your package add to, and extend, the play value of the toy?
- Does your package help the toy pop off the shelf?
- Does your package engage the child and the parent by inviting them to interact with the toy?
- Does your package help parents by providing important information about the toy's benefits, appropriateness, or safety?

CHAPTER 17

Creating the Next Blockbuster Toy

There is no magic formula to create the next blockbuster toy. Different people have made different discoveries over the years, many times based upon chance observations. Ruth Handler noted that there were no dolls her daughter could play with that could represent her daughter's budding aspirations, and so she created the Barbie doll. Charles Darrow noted during the Great Depression that people needed a well-deserved retreat to a get-rich fantasy, and so he created Monopoly. Binney & Smith thought about a utensil that would allow children to create masterpieces, and so they created Crayola Crayons. Each of these inventions then had to depend upon a plethora of other people and events, from retailers who believed in the toy enough to carry it, to positive public relations, to effective advertising, to children who would actually care enough about the toy to add it to millions of wish lists, and finally to parents who would find enough value in the toys that they would honor their children's requests.

This is not easy, nor is it ever guaranteed. That's why in the history of modern toymaking, there are a small number of truly blockbuster toys. Each and every year, the dominant toys tend to be those that were invented many decades ago. Every year there are only one or two truly new blockbuster toys, and many of those fade quickly and never become Ever-Cool, because they could not regenerate themselves year after year to reflect changing fads. They were too dependent upon a single fad or an entertainment property that has a limited shelf life. The numbers show it all. Approximately 7,000 new toy products are introduced each year. That means the chances of any given toy becoming a blockbuster are about 2 in 7,000, or 1 in 3,500. Not good. Even if you are lucky enough to have launched the blockbuster, the chances that it will be around in five years are almost zero. Thus, the odds that any particular toymaker will invent a truly new, long-lasting toy are slight.

But the odds of creating a blockbuster are increased significantly if certain guidelines are followed. I know this from experience. During my twenty-plus-year career, a lot of my time was spent nurturing existing toy brands, helping launch new line extensions of those brands, and helping launch truly new blockbuster toys. Much of this came from the many years I spent working for the advertising agency that handled the Mattel business, as well as the last five-plus years in my consulting practice. I worked on brands such as Barbie dolls, Hot Wheels vehicles, Cabbage Patch Kids, Polly Pocket, He-Man, as well as various toys based upon new Disney properties. Along the way, I made a note of those guidelines that can increase the odds of creating a blockbuster toy. We have discussed these guidelines throughout this book: being *on emotional target* with children and/or parents, being *on trend*, being *regenerative*, having *playful marketing*, and being fortunate enough to lay the right foundation for the unpredictable *X Factor*.

Such precepts are not ironclad, however, for guidelines should always be tested and broken. But it's helpful to learn from past experiences so that successful paths can be traveled and most mistakes can be avoided. What follows are some practical tools that toymakers can use to put the guidelines to work, thus increasing their odds of creating the Next Big Thing in blockbuster toys.

Creating Blockbuster Toy Ideas

It all begins with an idea, of course. But a lot of idea generation tends to be random. A toymaker may have a chance thought while in the shower, for example, for a great new toy. They might then bring the idea to life in sketches in hopes that others will care enough about the idea to devote resources to it. While such efforts will bear fruit on occasion, the odds favor a more structured and formal approach to ideation, one that nets both tonnage and quality. The more ideas generated within well-structured parameters, the more likely one of the ideas will be "sold" to other executives and eventually be made a success among children and parents.

I have used many tools to help toymakers in global companies generate ideas, but one of my favorites is the ideation matrix. A matrix simply puts on one sheet of paper the key elements (guidelines previously discussed in this book) that toymakers can use to generate potentially powerful ideas. An example of a toy matrix is in exhibit 5. The first column is an abbreviated list of toy categories that the toymaker may be investigating, such as infant and preschool toys, dolls, plush, and so forth. This is followed by column 2, which includes the key emotional needs for children (e.g., pride, power, silliness) and their parents (e.g., child's happiness, development, success). Column 3 identifies the ways that satisfying these emotional needs can help a child transform (e.g., into a master, creator, nurturer). These two columns (emotional needs and transformation) will help the toymaker ensure that toy ideas are *on emotional target*. In particular, they will help the toymaker ascertain if an emotional need is being ignored by competitors in a given category (column 1), thus representing an opportunity. Column 4 has a list of key features that will be used to support the emotional needs and transformation. This helps create the play pattern. Column 5 includes key, pervasive trends existing today. These will help the toymaker develop toys that are *on trend*. Column 6 lists the key marketing tools so that, as the toymaker is developing toy ideas, at least some attention can be given toward inventing ideas that naturally lead to *playful marketing*.

All of these columns have been addressed in this book, with the exception of column 5 (trends). The following is a brief

Exhibit 5
Creating Blockbuster Toys!

1. Toy Categories	2. Child Emotional Needs	3. Transformation	4. Features	5. Trends	6. Marketing
Infant & Preschool	Pride	Master	Shape	KGOY	Public Relations
Dolls	Self Esteem	Creator	Size	Pop Culture	Advertising
Plush	Appreciation/Admiration	Nurturer	Look	World Awareness	Sales Promotions
Action Figures	Accomplishment/mastery	Emulator	Sound	Premium On Time	Packaging
Vehicles	Creativity	Friend	Smell	Technology	Etc
Ride-ons	Beauty	Collector	Taste	Just for Me	
Games/Puzzles	Power	Story Lover	Texture	Empowerment	
Activity Toys	Control	Experience Seeker	Activation	"DO Something Products"	
Video Games	Silliness/Grossness	Etc	Etc	Experiences Galore	
Computer Games	Independence/Freedom			Category Overlaps	
	Belonging			Mystical/Magical/New Age	
Etc	To Nurture/Be Nurtured (loved)			15+ minutes of Fame	
-Water toys	Security			Girl Power	
-Musical	Overcome Fears/Bravery			Good To Be a Kid	
-Etc	Sensory Gratification			Americanism/Patriotism	
	Fantasy Fulfillment			Rainbow Culture	
	Hunger/Thirst			Rise of Grandparents	
	Etc			Etc	

Parent Emotional Needs
Child's Happiness
Child's Continued Enjoyment (play value)
Child's Safety
Child's Mental & Physical Development
Child's Success
Child's Health
Child's Love
Etc

Mix & Match Options from Left to Right

explanation of some of the key trends that exist today so that the toymaker can understand their scope and potential use. Once these trends are reviewed, the matrix will be demonstrated.

- *KGOY:* This refers to Kids Growing Older, at Younger ages. Children seem to be maturing faster than they did years ago. Today's seven- and eight-year-olds seem to be more aware of worldly things than children of similar ages a couple of decades ago. This is undoubtedly a result of many things, such as greater exposure to various media, and divorce rates, which remain substantial (creating more latchkey kids). Traditional toys, themselves, used to top out among children once they reached ages ten or eleven. Now they top out among children ages seven or eight. Only video and computer games have grown with children. Toymakers need to think about how to develop toys that appeal to this maturing sensibility.

- *Pop Culture:* Pop culture in music, sports, fashion, and so forth is moving to lower and lower ages. Toymakers need to think about how their toy concepts can connect with pop culture in ways children and parents will appreciate.

- *World Awareness:* Children know more about the world than ever before. This includes an awareness of wars, cultures, and customs. This is driven by the media, the schools, and the Internet. Toymakers need to think of the global child with global needs and global awareness.

- *Premium on Time:* Children are strapped for time. They are more involved in school and out-of-school activities (e.g., sports teams, music lessons, computer/Internet, etc.) than ever before. As a result, toys do not just compete with other toys; they compete with all other activities a child may partake in. Toymakers need to think about how new toy ideas can compete with these broader activities.

- *Technology:* Technology of all sorts is encroaching on children's lives, from cell phones, Internet, and virtual reality to simple technology buzzes that add sounds, lights, and so forth to products void of such things. Toymakers need to think about how they can bring these elements into a child's world, as well as how they can make common things special by adding technological touches.

- *Just for Me:* More and more products in a child's world allow them to tailor it to their preferences. Toymakers need to consider how they can help children customize their toys to reflect individual tastes.
- *Empowerment:* Children are feeling more and more empowered, thanks to many of the aforementioned trends. Toymakers need to think about ways that their toys can empower children, perhaps by making them feel more in control of their world than ever before.
- *DO Something Products:* As mentioned in an earlier chapter, "do something" products are growing. Toymakers need to ask this question of all their toys: "What does it do?" But the answer must always be in context of the core emotional needs it seeks to satisfy. Random elements (bells and whistles) that do not support the overall brand purpose add confusion.
- *Experiences Galore:* Children are being offered more exciting experiences than ever, from amusement parks to malls, the Internet, and so on. Toymakers might be able to tap into this by making common things special, as cited earlier, or by providing a greater sense of adventure through the introduction of more story-based toys.
- *Category Overlaps:* More categories are beginning to blur. Toymakers need to think about how they can build toylike properties into other categories, ranging from foods to apparel. It's all playable.
- *Mystical/Magical/New Age:* This trend has been evident since the new century approached and has found its way into stories (e.g., Buffy the Vampire Slayer, Harry Potter) and products. Toymakers should consider investigating these themes.
- *Fifteen-Plus Minutes of Fame:* Technology allows children to be made famous, and more and more manufacturers, through promotions, Internet exposure, and such, are giving children

their fifteen minutes of fame. Can you invent a toy that facilitates this?

• *Girl Power:* Started decades ago, this trend is still prevalent. Toymakers need to think about how their toys can empower girls. Yet girls will still embrace the traditional themes (beauty, nurturing, etc.). How the toymaker connects with the "whole" girl will be the future mantra.

• *Good to Be a Kid:* Despite children's greater awareness of the world and the fact that they seem to be maturing faster, more and more children seem to want to stay kids longer. They don't seem to want to grow up too fast, yet they want adult "things" such as cell phone, cars, etc. Toymakers need to think about how they can accommodate a child's need to be a kid in a world in which they often grow up too quickly.

• *Americanism/Patriotism:* Since the tragic events of 9/11, followed by the war with Iraq, American adults have embraced a renewed sense of patriotism, and so have their sons and daughters. It's unclear whether this heightened patriotism will become a long-term trend. But toymakers might consider how they can help children express that patriotism in ways that are acceptable to parents and not exploitative (that goes for all these trends).

• *Rainbow Culture:* Children, more and more, represent all colors of the rainbow. These cultures are rich in history, values, and customs. Toymakers need to invent toys that reflect children's growing exposure to and delight in diversity.

• *Rise of Grandparents:* Grandparents not only account for a good deal of toy purchases, but many have become more involved with raising their grandchildren when the child's parents get divorced (still a significant issue for many children). Toymakers need to better understand how this might impact toy concepts and marketing.

Matrix in Use

The matrix simply helps the toymaker generate potential toy ideas. It does so by helping the toymaker combine various items on the list, looking for opportunities that are *on emotional target, on trend, regenerative* over time, while using *playful marketing*. The following are some examples of how the matrix might be used. Some of these ideas may, in the history of toys, have already been tried successfully or otherwise. The point of these examples is simply to demonstrate how to utilize the matrix for ideation. For example:

• *Idea:* From the first column (Toy Categories), we can begin our ideation session by inventing a new push and pull preschool toy. From the second column (Emotional Needs), we can decide to make this toy idea satisfy a child's need for a little control. From the third column (Transformation), we may decide to combine this with the child's love of stories. From the fourth column (Features), we can fulfill this transformation by making the toy tell a story (Sound) when the child pulls it along the floor. Thus, the child has control over starting and stopping the story by starting and stopping pulling the toy. We might sell different cartridges for the toy so that the parent only has to buy it once, and then can buy the various cartridges to provide more stories for the child. To keep the toy current over time, the new cartridges can reflect timeless stories, or ones that dovetail with contemporary entertainment properties, or ones that dovetail with key items from the fifth column (Trends, such as Empowerment, World Awareness, etc.). That will keep it *on trend* and *regenerative*. We might add stories with strong educational components, ranging from friendship to ABCs, thus helping parents in their quest to guide their child. From the sixth column (Marketing), we might use popular characters or famous actors as the storytellers, to make the toy newsworthy (Public Relations). One option could be for the parent to be able to record their own voice telling the story, giving them greater involvement. The package should be created so that the child can pull the toy in-store, thus to experiencing the plaything. We can call this idea *Pull Tales*.

• *Idea:* Or we can take a Computer Game, satisfy children's need for Fantasy Fulfillment, and transform them into Emulators (*on emotional target*). The Features include a CD-ROM that allows children to scan in photos of themselves. The program then *ages* the child's face to estimate what the child will look like at age twenty-one, thirty-five, forty-five, and so forth. That will put it *on trend,* technologically. It will also allow kids to experience a day as one of a dozen professionals they might become: a doctor, newspaper reporter, secret agent, candy-store operator, or even president of the United States. The better the child handles both the mundane events of the profession and the "surprise/emergency events," the more points they rack up. We can keep it contemporary each year by expanding the professions available. We might even launch it into the online multiplayer environment so that children can interact with others who are also playing roles of different professionals (technology trend). It differs from other online games in that children get to use older images of themselves. Marketing wise, we might have famous professionals endorse the game, perhaps even making cameo appearances in the CD-ROM. We might also have a kiosk in-store so that the child can take a photo of himself and immediately see his face *age up* as he might appear in the game. We might also have contests where the winner gets paid tuition at a college of their choice. We can title it *Future ME CD.*

• *Idea:* Or we can select a Ride-on (bike) and decide to make it in a way to satisfy a child's desire for Creativity by transforming him into a Master builder and mechanic. The Features will allow children to "build" the bike in hundreds of different configurations by mixing some twenty different components. The mixing and matching alters both the bike's appearance (challenge: which appearance looks the hottest?) and its ability to race (challenge: which configuration is the fastest?). Marketing wise, we might have local and national competitions for the hottest and fastest bikes. The bikes themselves might have been designed by the most popular BMX racers, thus adding credibility. Call it *Bike Max*.

Whether you hate these ideas or love them doesn't matter. The point is simply this: the matrix can help the would-be inventor generate literally hundreds of ideas by simply laying before the toymakers' eyes various elements to be mixed and matched. This will give toymakers more options to consider before they narrow the ideas to a more manageable and higher-potential few. The selection process is typically simple:

- Which ideas are the most unique?
- Which ideas truly connect with strong *emotional needs*?
- Which ideas are *on trend*?
- Which ideas can more easily be reinvented each year to connect with trends and fads to become Ever-Cool (*regenerative*)?
- Which ideas lend themselves naturally to the creation of blockbuster, *playful marketing*?

The last point is as critical as the first. The reason that the final column in exhibit 5 contains the marketing elements is so that toymakers can challenge themselves to see if the idea is easily extended into marketing. The longer the marketing legs and the more a toymaker can "see" the exciting implications of the toy idea, the more likely it is that the toy idea can be "sold" to those the toymaker must depend upon (e.g., other company executives, distributors, and eventually consumers).

Though the matrix in exhibit 5 is a rather simple one, it is filled with thousands of configurations that lead to thousands of potential ideas; you simply have to find them by mixing and matching options. More complex matrices can be constructed that would include many more toy categories, lists of key childhood fantasies, new technologies, themes children enjoy (space, dinosaurs, magic, etc.), and various leisure activities that compete for a child's time (sports, theme parks, etc.). These will greatly expand the number of options that can be created. When generating toy ideas based upon upcoming entertainment properties, the toymaker might also list the key characters, storylines (good vs. evil, etc.), accessories used in the film (magic wands, vehicles, etc.), and specific scenes from the movie that the child might recreate at home (e.g., scene when heroes triumph).

Though the matrix approach and other ideation techniques will not guarantee a blockbuster, they will help tremendously by bringing a formalized approach to the process.

Creating Blockbuster Playthings in Everything

As mentioned in chapter 11, toylike properties are fast becoming a central part of many blockbuster nontoy products. Exhibit 6 is merely one way to generate ideas that give other products toylike qualities. As with the previous matrix, the would-be developer simply mixes and matches elements in this matrix to generate ideas. These ideas would then be culled down, researched, and, if the potential is found, introduced into the marketplace. Some examples:

• *Idea:* A food manufacturer might select a Snack (say cookies), mix it with a toy category (say Action Figures), combine it with emotional needs (say Power and Hunger satisfaction), and finally decide to transform the child into an Emulator. The cookies can be in the Shape of new action-figure characters. Every box comes with the good characters and the villains so that children can stage mock battles and "eat" those who are vanquished in the "crunch" of battle. Marketing wise, each box might also have a comic strip on the back that routinely updates the exploits of the characters, so as to connect with the child's love of stories while helping the brand stay regenerative over time. New characters (and cookies) might get added on occasion to enhance appeal and novelty. We might even add popular action-oriented characters (real and fanciful) to make the product newsworthy. Call it *Cookie Crunch*.

• *Idea:* A developer might select a Fast-Food Restaurant, Vehicles, Fantasy Fulfillment, and again Emulator. To fulfill

Exhibit 6
Creating a Plaything in Everything!

1. Non-Toy Categories	2. Toy Categories	3. Child Emotional Needs	4. Transformation	5. Features
	Infant & Preschool			
Snacks	Dolls	Pride	Master	Shape
-candy		Self Esteem	Creator	Size
-potato chips	Plush	Appreciation/Admiration	Nurturer	Look
-etc		Accomplishment/mastery	Emulator	Sound
	Action Figures	Creativity	Friend	Smell
Beverages		Beauty	Collector	Taste
-colas	Vehicles	Power	Story Lover	Texture
-100% juices		Control	Experience Seeker	Activation
-drinks	Ride-ons	Silliness/Grossness	Etc	Etc
-etc		Independence/Freedom		
	Games/Puzzles	Belonging		
Packaged Meats		To Nurture/Be Nurtured (loved)		
	Activity Toys	Security		
Fast Food Restaurants		Overcome Fears/Bravery		
	Video Games	Sensory Gratification		
School Supplies		Fantasy Fulfillment		
	Computer Games	Hunger/Thirst		
Theme Parks		Etc		
	Etc			
Beauty Care	-Water toys	**Parent Emotional Needs**		
	-Musical	Child's Happiness		
Sports Equipment	-Etc	Child's Continued Enjoyment (play value)		
		Child's Safety		
Apparel		Child's Mental & Physical Development		
		Child's Success		
Etc		Child's Health		
		Child's Love		
		Etc		

this transformation, the restaurant might have booths that are shaped like cars (dragsters, etc.) that the child and parents jump into and can be served in. Each car comes with a steering wheel, working windshield wipers, etc. The cars have a multiplayer video game that allows the child to drive and race with other kids in other cars as they dine. Marketing wise, we might tie into a racecar organization (e.g., NASCAR) or give points for children and parents who win races, redeemable during future restaurant trips. Call it *Fast Foods.*

- *Idea:* A developer might select the Snack category (this time potato chips). Add Sensory Gratification whereby the chip is a natural color in the bag but turns into bright colors when you begin to eat it. It can connect with the child's desire for Independence/Freedom (safe rebellion) by positioning the chip as rebellious. Marketing wise, the advertising will show the highly demonstrable color change. To keep it contemporary, we might add new colors over time, perhaps a sound (fizz chips!), and more. These are chips with attitude. Call them *Rebel Chips.*

- *Idea:* A toymaker may decide that he wishes to bring his expertise of making dolls into the Beverage world. So he crafts colorful glass bottles that look like spunky teenagers, complete with molded heads that look real. The head screws off the bottle top so that the girl can consume the beverage (a peppy, sparkling soda with extra calcium to help girls grow). The bottle also comes with high-quality, hot fashion accessories that allow girls to dress the bottles up (you can't even tell there's a bottle underneath). The bottles become collectibles. To keep the product contemporary, the bottle "heads" can even be crafted in the guise of female icons from current pop culture. Call it *Sparkles!*

Once again, these ideas were created simply to provide a sense of how the matrices can be used. They formalize a process that is often haphazard, leading to a greater abundance of ideas.

Ask Kids and Parents

Those ideas that meet the initial criteria of uniqueness, satisfaction of a strong *emotional need*, being *on trend*, and having potential for Ever-Cool status (*regenerative*), while lending themselves to *playful marketing*, can be culled down and sent into research to ascertain which have the most potential. Since children are eventually going to vote with their requests, and parents are eventually going to vote with their approval, executives might as well get their opinions earlier rather than later.

There are many ways to research toys to ascertain their blockbuster potential. One of the most effective is to allow children and parents to select from the new toy ideas (in illustration or prototype form, depending upon the nature of the toy) and those that are current blockbusters in the market. This will help the toymaker judge the new idea's true potential relative to competitive offerings and discover any concerns that might exist among children or their parents. Several books, including my earlier *Creating Ever-Cool* discuss key aspects of research, so I won't repeat that here. But plenty of tools are available to help weed out the toys that do not have potential, while narrowing the list to those that do.

The Next Big Thing: Basic Principles

• The toymaker's challenge is to create a formal process for generating a multitude of ideas that are *on emotional target, on trend,* and *regenerative,* while inspiring *playful marketing.*

CHAPTER 18

Creating Destiny

In the earliest of times, toys were more than just playthings. When parents in ancient Rome gave their children toy soldiers, it was about teaching children the rudiments of battle, which would become an important part of their lives. It was a warrior state, and for better or worse, they groomed warriors. When parents in the New World gave their daughters baby dolls, it was about teaching them about parenthood. Our world—at least the more civilized parts of our world—has changed in many ways. Yet even to this day, boys still play with action figures, as will some girls, and both will pretend to thwart evil in the world. They will also both play with nurturing toys of one sort or another to practice being a parent.

I believe that in both small and grand ways, playing with toys can have an important impact upon our children. Children learn, develop, emulate, practice, share, and have fun . . . all through their interaction with toys. A great many resources and studies state the same. In the book *Dr. Toy's Smart Play,* author Stevanne Auerbach cites research that shows that "toys stimulate 25 percent more brain synapses per neuron," and "children who do not play and are rarely touched have brains that are 20 to 30 percent smaller than normal for their age." Infants and toddlers can increase their eye and hand coordination and problem-solving skills through play with toys, while older children can learn more about socialization, role play, and future vocations. I am willing to bet that there are female doctors today who played with a Doctor Barbie doll when they were young and were inspired by it. I am willing to bet that there are architects today who played with Erector Sets when they were young while wondering what it would be like to build skyscrapers in the real world. I believe that there are generals today who, when young, played with G.I. Joe action figures while pretending to safeguard a nation. That's not to say that every child who plays with an action hero will become a general or that every child who plays a game of chess will become a grandmaster. It's to say that every child who plays also *experiences something* in the process, and that these subtle experiences can shape minds, which shapes lives. Toys help a child *feel something*, which leads to joy and happiness and optimism and emotional fulfillment. This is an awesome responsibility for anyone involved in the creation of a plaything.

Toymakers do not just create smiles but, in a way, can help shape *destiny*, even ever so slightly. I truly believe this; toys can help shape destiny. It's true that any given toy's full impact on a child is probably quite small relative to other far more prevalent factors such as genetics, parental involvement, home life, and friends. Yet even a small impact can carry a degree of responsibility. And with it, there are many dilemmas. If a toymaker introduces a new action hero, is this nurturing more aggressiveness in our society or is it teaching children to "play" being a hero who is not afraid to stand up to evil aggressors around the world? If a toymaker creates a beauty fashion doll, is this fostering too great an emphasis on outer beauty or is it simply allowing the child to play out a harmless fantasy?

These issues never leave us. In an earlier book I wrote entitled *A Knight's Code of Business,* which addressed issues of character and competence in the corporate world, I mentioned that I am forever faced with issues that challenge character. "How can we make millions of children smile," I said in that book, "without rotting their teeth in the process? How do we make millions of children laugh, without rotting their minds in the process?" All toymakers need to keep these issues at the forefront to ensure that the toys and marketing they provide children far outweigh the potential downside.

What follows are issues that toymakers and marketers face, updated from my previous writings. These issues are not easily resolved, for most depend not upon objective measures but subjective ones.

Marketing to Kids

Some people would prefer that marketers never design any products for children (toys or otherwise), never talk to kids via advertising, and never entice a child with a special offer or promotion. They see marketing as exploitation, plain and simple, of our youth. This is the most extreme view and doesn't fully appreciate the benefits of making and selling toys.

The simple role of toymaking is to invent playthings that fulfill needs. In a child's case, this includes the needs for mastery, nurturing, emulation, creation, accomplishment, and so on. Most parents can attest to the hours of smiles that a simple yo-yo can bring to the child's face, the feeling of accomplishment that can come from a work of art molded from Play-Doh modeling compound, or the tender feelings of comfort that arise as a child embraces her Cabbage Patch Kids. Such toys provide not only fun for the child, but also greater convenience for the parent who may not have the time or the skill to construct these toys by hand. Most would agree, then, that the existence of such manufactured toys is beneficial.

Regarding the appropriateness of advertising and marketing toys directly to children, parents often offer up a range of opinions. Some feel that advertising and marketing set unrealistic temptations, foster materialism, and create conflict in the home as children are motivated to make requests. Others have told me that advertising and marketing to kids is acceptable because it simply provides information about what is available. And providing they do so accurately, such efforts are even viewed as a learning experience for when those children become adults themselves. Some studies suggest that this is true. The 1999 Nickelodeon/Yankelovich Youth Monitor study revealed that only 25 percent of kids ages nine to seventeen trusted TV commercials. Clearly, parents and perhaps past experience have made children cautious about what is being advertised. Still, there are European countries that prohibit advertising to children. A key issue they cite is that children under twelve do not understand what advertising is, and as a result it creates an unfair advantage for the advertiser. They do allow advertising for kids' products, but only if directed to parents. In such an environment, parents undoubtedly have to get their child's input anyway to help them figure out what the child wants. So children are probably exposed to marketing via parent-directed advertising, in-store efforts, and friends.

Parents are also becoming more and more critical of the quantity of kids' products and their advertising. This becomes most pronounced when movie franchises are launched, complete with a toy, cereals, candy bars, bed sheets, a kid's meal, and so on. While this is the reality of today's toy marketplace, toymakers must be careful not to overcommercialize toys. Interestingly enough, marketplace forces are at work here. Parents have become less willing to buy into each new franchise. This places a greater burden on toymakers to develop toys that are truly innovative in the eyes of both children and their parents. That's a good thing for the industry.

While some parents would like less advertising, overall, it can come at a price. One study found that television-advertised toys are actually sold at lower prices than toys that are not advertised on television. That's for many reasons, most notably because retailers use television-advertised toys to get people in the store. The large volume of buyers generated by television also lowers the manufacturing costs per item, which carries over into a lower retail price. Some economic theories also suggest that a ban on advertising actually creates an unfair advantage toward existing brands because they are the ones that already have awareness, and that new brands are handicapped because they do not have advertising as a means to create awareness. So while consumers want less "marketing," it can come with a price: higher prices and less innovation.

But I, too, can get tired of dealing with my own children's requests that come from their exposure to advertised toys. Because I'm a marketer, however, I do appreciate the fact that a child's request is the result of a toymaker doing a good job of offering toys that satisfy my children's emotional needs. In fact, for each child request, I remind myself that there are a multitude of other toys that will fail because my children, and millions of others, did not request them. More often than not, the winning toymaker simply took the time and spent the resources to understand my children's needs.

This is not to say that all marketing directed to children is good. It's not. In the race to fulfill a child's needs, things can go wrong. Toys may not be safe. Advertising may be misleading. Promotions may use unreasonable pressure. All of this means that while toymaking and marketing to children, in general, can be beneficial to kids and parents alike, we still need to be watchdogs in the specifics. We must ensure that, on our way to help create smiles and to shape destiny in some small way, the benefits of a toy far outweigh the potential negatives of its marketing program.

Product Safety

Toys must be safe for the child to play with. In the toy arena, the Consumer Product Safety Commission sends field inspectors to monitor the marketplace, searching for toys that might pose electrical, thermal, mechanical, chemical, or flammable hazards. Specific toy safety standards include requirements for such items as surface-coating material, toy-cap noise levels, sharp edges and points, and small parts that could be swallowed or inhaled. There are approximately 100 separate tests and design specifications in the federal regulations, all in an attempt to safeguard children. There are also requirements for package labeling so that parents are warned of potential dangers, such as choking hazards.

When toymakers violate such rules, their toys are sent back for changes. If a toy actually makes it to market and harms a child, then toy companies must be held accountable. Toymakers should have a solemn oath: *Make children happy, safely*.

Product Quality

Toys must be of quality, for quality does matter—so much so that manufacturers seldom profit from making a product of poor quality. In a launch of a new toy some years ago, 25 percent of the toys were returned because they simply did not work properly. This proved devastating for the manufacturer. Not only did it hurt their credibility among consumers but among retailers as well. As such, toymakers must include safeguards to ensure their products will be well received. They must conduct tests to ensure that a child can play or activate a toy in a manner desired without breakage. Through all of this, manufacturers must weigh not just quality but price/value, for parents are many times not willing or able to pay a higher price commensurate with the highest-quality product. So the best quality, at the most affordable price, is often the goal. This perceived quality and price ratio (value), and more specifically, play value, is all important. The more time a child spends playing with your toy, the more the parent will appreciate it, and the more it will be deemed to offer value. That helps create long-term toy brands. If the child does not play with the toy long enough or often enough, the parent will be leery about buying related toy items from the line. Quality matters, and in the toy world, that means not only that it doesn't break, but that it has play longevity.

Advertising

As mentioned earlier, the toymaker must accurately communicate the performance of the toy to its audience. It behooves the toymaker to communicate well, not only because it is the right thing to do, but because children are skeptical to begin with, which creates the need to go above and beyond in accurately portraying the toy.

There are also organizations in place that are watching. The Children's Advertising Review Unit (CARU), which is part of the Council of Better Business Bureaus, was established in 1974 by the advertising industry in order to promote responsible children's advertising. Its function is to review and evaluate advertising directed to children under twelve years of age. If it finds advertising to be in conflict with its guidelines, it seeks changes through the advertiser's voluntary cooperation. The CARU guidelines provide many specific parameters that advertising should follow related to such elements as copy, sound, visual presentations, environments, product demonstrations, and violence. The guidelines go on to outline practices related to the use of extreme sales pressure, disclosures and disclaimers, comparative claims, celebrity endorsements, premiums, promotions, and sweepstakes. For example, advertisements should not suggest that children would be more popular if they owned a toy, they should not urge the child to ask their parent to buy a toy, and toys that arise out of a television program should not be advertised during or adjacent to the program. In addition to CARU guidelines, the television networks impose guidelines on advertisers to ensure that a toy is accurately portrayed, is displayed in a safe play environment, and is demonstrated in the context of its merit as a toy and that the advertising discloses the toy's operation, package contents, and assembly and battery requirements. At times, the Federal Trade Commission will also get involved and prevent the advertiser from using certain techniques. Federal law also limits the amount of television advertising that can be directed to children in an hour. The intent of all these efforts is to ensure that toys are portrayed accurately, that the benefits communicated are not overpromised, that the amount of television advertising is limited, and that children are not harmed.

It's very important, too, to realize that advertising that attempts to show the child "transform" into fanciful personas, such as a mother, superhero, and so forth, must make it clear that such transformations are purely in the realm of fantasy, so that younger children do not mistakenly think they might transform into such personas in reality. The line between fantasy and reality must be made apparent at all times, taking into account the maturity of the intended audience.

In the development of a toy commercial I worked on many years ago, concern was raised that the fantasy elements in the advertisement would make children believe a toy would do things it could not do. So we tested the spot among children, discovered there was slight miscommunication, and fixed it before it ever went on the air. That's simply how the issues should be addressed. Toymakers must be in it for the long term, which means setting accurate expectations of what the toy can deliver. Overpromising a toy's performance is not only morally dubious, it is not a sound business practice, as many toys will be returned, children will be disappointed, and both retailers and parents will be angry.

Aggressive Play and Mature Subjects

Parents are more and more concerned over children's exposure to overly aggressive and mature subject matter, made even greater, some say, by some toymakers. For many years, critics have argued that toy guns should not be sold because they supposedly preach violence to children. More recently, video-game manufacturers have been taken to task for the violence and sexual depictions in some games. "Violence is a staple in the adolescent world of video games while sex traditionally has been taboo," reported the *Los Angeles Times* in October 2002. "But a decade after Acclaim Entertainment Inc. rattled parents with the hyper-violent 'Mortal Kombat' series, the publisher again is pushing the boundaries of taste and propriety—this time by spicing up its 'BMX XXX' with topless female bicycle riders, a racy script and video clips of strippers."

What parent could read that statement and not be alarmed, particularly since many adults still think of video games as a child's toy? But the truth is that the increase in violence and mature subject matter is a reflection of the aging of game players. It's estimated that more than half of all Sony's PlayStation 2 players are now older than eighteen. While video games began their existence as a "kid's thing," these kids have refused to leave their games behind as they become adults. Much like television and movies, then, the video-game environment is quickly becoming a medium for all audiences. For these same reasons, video-game manufacturers have begun to provide ratings on their products, just as movies are rated, so that parents can be alerted to the mature themes and retailers can be alerted as to who can and cannot buy their games. Games rated M, for example, are restricted to purchasers by those seventeen and older. Games rated AO are for adults only. Still, for all the excitement they create in the press, M-rated games remain a small part of the market, at about 10 percent. Even the controversial game "BMX XXX" experienced "lackluster sales" according to one source in early 2003. For all the controversy that mature games generate, the money in the industry still remains with those games that both children and parents accept. That's a good thing, too.

Toymakers must ensure that their games are rated appropriately and that they do not knowingly advertise mature games to audiences they are not intended for, and retailers must be sure they do not sell games to anyone who is underage.

Yet it's not that easy in the trenches. Let's say a new movie is introduced that has heroes and villains and battle scenes. Let's say a toy line is introduced based upon that movie. Let's say the manufacturer conducts a survey and 80 percent of parents are okay with their children of a certain age playing with these toys. Should the toymaker make the toys? Clearly, if 80 percent of parents do not object, the toymaker might feel it is acceptable to make the toys. However, they are apt to hear from the remaining, highly vocal 20 percent of parents who are not happy about it. Let's say the opposite occurs, and the piece of entertainment and the toys derived from it are acceptable to only 20 percent of the parents. Should the toymaker make the toys to fulfill the needs of those 20 percent, even by giving the toys an appropriate rating, or should those 20 percent be denied? This is the world the toymaker lives in. And these questions cannot be so easily answered or dismissed. But sales volume is typically on the side of social consciousness. Once again, the games that do best are often those that both kids like and parents accept (either actively or through indifference).

Some social researchers say that entertainment that has aggressive depictions leads some children to act more aggressively. Others state that such research used flawed methodologies, that "aggressive" play behavior cannot be construed as a precursor to actual "violent" behavior, and that toys used in aggressive play can actually have a beneficial effect by helping children release daily frustrations. In his book *Killing Monsters,* Gerard Jones stated, "Becoming a warrior or a superhero able to beat any bad guy is a generic but thrilling 'new ending' to all the everyday stories of not being old enough or powerful enough to make things come out the way children want." After exhaustively reviewing the academic literature that purports that aggressive toys create aggressive children, he went on to assert, "There is no evidence to support the fear that videogames have increased the amount or changed the nature of crime anywhere." Children who commit violent acts have troubling issues at home or in their environment that shape their destiny far more than toys can. Still, the notion that a toy might ever so slightly shape a negative destiny should be considered when developing toys.

It should never be forgotten, too, that while marketers, the government, consumer advocates, and special-interest groups all play important roles, the greatest role of all is played by the individual parent or caregiver who has the ultimate responsibility for a child's upbringing. They have the ability to veto those toys they deem harmful and to guide their children in a manner that reflects their beliefs and moral judgments. In this world of numerous playthings and ample marketing, it does mean that a parent's job is both increasingly important and increasingly difficult. Children will at times ask for toys that their parents feel are inappropriate. The best thing a parent can do when faced with this dilemma is this: don't buy the toy! The child will learn from the experience, and so will the toy-maker.

The Legacy of Blockbuster Toys

This book began with a simple premise, that blockbuster toys help children transform in subtle, fun ways. This book ends with a simple notion, that all toys, and most notably blockbuster toys due to their ubiquity, have an equally subtle—and limited—hand in shaping destiny. That gives toys both meaning and scope. Perhaps that, more than anything, explains why toys were with mankind from the beginning and why they will stay with us until the very end.

Because of this, the most important ingredient in a toy is trust—trust that children will like it and parents will appreciate it. "Because so many of today's parents grew up with Disney themselves, there is an inherent trust built into the brand," says Matt Ryan, senior vice-president of corporate brand management at The Walt Disney Company. "They count on Disney to do the right thing. When it comes to making products, we put on our 'parent hats' and try to make toys and activities that reinforce the positive values parents expect from Disney." That, perhaps, is the most important test of all. Toymakers need to wear their kid's cap when developing a toy to ensure they take into account children's needs, but they must also put on their parent's cap to ensure they take into account the parents' needs.

Toymakers, whether they work at a bench in the basement or in the boardroom in a skyscraper, have both a profound opportunity and a profound responsibility. They have the potential to do great good. It comes down to one question. Can you state with pride that your toy not only helps children have fun and is safe, of quality, and accurately communicated but also has the power to help millions of children around the world grow, learn, express, think, wonder, face fears, emulate, master, create, nurture, or experience the world on an unprecedented scale? If so, you have created not just any toy but a blockbuster toy, whose legacy will live not merely in the company's accounting ledger, but in the hearts and minds of countless generations of children and their appreciative parents. You have made smiles.

Toy Index